10 Minutes to Better Body Image

also in the 10 Minutes to Better Mental Health series

10 Minutes to Better Mental Health
A Step-by-Step Guide for Teens Using CBT and Mindfulness
Lee David and Debbie Brewin
Illustrated by Rebecca Price
ISBN 978 1 78775 556 7
eISBN 978 1 78775 570 3

10 Minutes to Beat Anxiety and Panic
A Step-by-Step Guide for Teens Using CBT and Mindfulness
Lee David and Debbie Brewin
Illustrated by Rebecca Price
ISBN 978 1 83997 848 7
eISBN 978 1 83997 849 4

10 Minutes to Boost Your Mood
A Step-by-Step Guide for Teens Using CBT and Mindfulness
Lee David and Debbie Brewin
Illustrated by Rebecca Price
ISBN 978 1 83997 895 1
eISBN 978 1 83997 896 8

of related interest

No Weigh!
A Teen's Guide to Positive Body Image, Food, and Emotional Wisdom
Shelley Aggarwal, Signe Darpinian, Wendy Sterling
Foreword by Connie Sobczak
ISBN 978 1 78592 825 3
eISBN 978 1 78450 946 0

Banish Your Body Image Thief
A Cognitive Behavioural Therapy Workbook on Building Positive Body Image for Young People
Kate Collins-Donnelly
ISBN 978 1 84905 463 8
eISBN 978 1 78450 946 0

10 MINUTES TO BETTER BODY IMAGE

A Step-by-Step Guide for Teens Using CBT and Mindfulness

Lee David and Debbie Brewin

Illustrated by Rebecca Price

Jessica Kingsley Publishers
London and Philadelphia

First published in Great Britain in 2025 by Jessica Kingsley Publishers
An imprint of John Murray Press

1

This book is intended to convey information to the reader. It is not intended for medical diagnosis or treatment. The reader should seek appropriate professional care and attention for any specific healthcare needs.

A CIP catalogue record for this title is available from the British Library and the Library of Congress

ISBN 978 1 83997 891 3
eISBN 978 1 83997 892 0

Printed and bound in Great Britain by Bell & Bain Limited

Jessica Kingsley Publishers' policy is to use papers that are natural, renewable and recyclable products and made from wood grown in sustainable forests. The logging and manufacturing processes are expected to conform to the environmental regulations of the country of origin.

Jessica Kingsley Publishers
Carmelite House
50 Victoria Embankment
London EC4Y 0DZ

www.jkp.com

John Murray Press
Part of Hodder & Stoughton Limited
An Hachette UK Company

The authorised representative in the EEA is Hachette Ireland,
8 Castlecourt Centre, Dublin 15, D15 XTP3, Ireland (email: info@hbgi.ie)

Contents

Introduction

→ Do you constantly worry about how you look in photos on social media and compare yourself negatively with others?

→ Have you ever felt upset or ashamed about your body or been the target of unkind or unhelpful comments about your appearance?

→ Does worrying about how you look affect your confidence and enjoyment of life, or stop you from doing things you want to do?

→ Have you got 10 minutes? Keep reading to find out how to build a better body image.

Sydney: I'm the tallest in my year and I've always felt lanky and awkward. My sisters are both petite and glamourous and often tease me about my height. They don't mean to upset me, but it really hurts my feelings. My social media is full of photos of people looking slim and gorgeous, all going out and having fun. I take loads of selfies but can't bring myself to post any photos because I never think I look good enough. I avoid going to parties because I worry that I don't look right or fit in. It's making me feel down, dull and boring, and it's definitely affecting my confidence.

Ross: I've always enjoyed sports and was picked for the athletics team due to my lean build, speed and agility. Lately, a lot of my friends seem to have grown taller, broader and more muscular. I keep thinking I look really small and weak compared to them, and they make jokes like patting me on the head, which makes me feel uncomfortable and embarrassed about my size. These days, I avoid hanging out with that group of friends, and I get stuck at home on my own in case the name-calling starts or they make me the focus of attention.

What is body image?

'Body image' refers to how you think and feel about your own body. How you imagine yourself in your own mind is personal and can be very different to how others see you. It may be a true and accurate reflection of your appearance but can also be distorted or unkind, and is often influenced by the unrealistic standards of beauty represented in advertising and social media.

Your body image can affect your mental health. Being overly critical of your appearance can lead to feelings of anxiety or shame. On the other hand, accepting and appreciating your body can make you feel confident and content in your own skin.

When does body image become a problem?

Feeling dissatisfied with your appearance from time to time is normal. You might sometimes worry about whether your hair is behaving or whether your shirt covers your tummy. It's natural to want to look good when meeting new friends or going out. However, when these concerns take over your life, affecting your happiness and friendships, it's time to take action.

Body image concerns have become common among teenagers and young adults. This is a stage of life where your body is developing and changing, and you are seeking out and exploring your own unique identity. These changes bring many complex emotions and uncertainties. At the same time, you are being bombarded with unhelpful messages through advertising, TV, movies and social media about what is considered beautiful or desirable, often created or enhanced by filters or other technology. This presents beauty standards that are unrealistic and impossible to match in the real world and which leave many people feeling inadequate and self-conscious.

Focusing too much on how you look can lead to stress, anxiety and low self-esteem. It can even trigger mental health problems such as eating disorders or depression. You can lose confidence and avoid social situations, becoming lonely and isolated. You may find yourself living a life that lacks interest, fun or enjoyment.

You are not alone...

It can help to remember that many of your peers are facing similar struggles with body image concerns. A survey of British teenagers (Mental Health Foundation 2019) found that millions worry about their body image sometimes and *over a third of young people worry about it often or every day.* It also found that:

→   Teenagers felt upset or ashamed about their body image.

→ Images on social media caused them to worry about their appearance.

→ Over a third stopped eating or restricted their diets at times due to worries about body image.

→ Many said that comments from friends made them worry about how they looked.

These concerns are echoed globally, with similar statistics and results from studies in different countries across the world.

How is your body image?

Let's start to think about your body image and how you see yourself. Recognizing that you have body image concerns is an important first step to building body confidence. Complete the table below:

Body image concerns	Have you noticed this often or very often in the past two weeks?
Do you feel unhappy or dissatisfied with certain aspects of your appearance?	
Do you compare your body or appearance to others?	
Do you frequently check how you look in mirrors or photos?	
Do you use cosmetics or clothing to hide aspects of your appearance?	
Do you believe it's crucial to look flawless for acceptance and success?	
Do you seek reassurance from others about your appearance but struggle to believe it?	
Do you use negative words like odd, weird, ugly, defective, unattractive or horrible to describe yourself?	
Are you considering surgery or other cosmetic procedures to fix the problems you see with your body?	
Do you feel anxious, fed up, low or ashamed because of how you look?	
Are you missing out on important things such as socializing, relationships, school or work because of appearance concerns?	

If you have answered often or very often to three or more of these body image concerns, then it may be time to think about ways to develop your body confidence and work towards a healthier, more positive relationship with your body.

What can you do?

Even though the influences of the media and society can be tough to change, there are steps you can take to feel better about yourself and to boost your body confidence. Why not start by picking up this book and doing the activities inside?

We will explore how to make friends with and accept your body, shifting your focus away from appearance and on to other important parts of life. Your self-worth extends far beyond just your physical looks!

By embracing your unique qualities and talents and respecting your body, you'll build the confidence and inner strength to live an exciting, interesting and meaningful life without allowing body image concerns to get in the way.

When to seek help

Body image concerns can have a major impact on your wellbeing and may sometimes be linked with mental health conditions such as eating disorders, body dysmorphic disorder, depression or self-harm.

If worries about your body image are having a severe effect on your mood or eating patterns, or if you are feeling hopeless or having thoughts of harming yourself, then we would strongly recommend that you talk to a trusted adult and seek professional help and support from your doctor.

We have also included some information about where to seek help in the 'Getting Support' section at the end of this book.

How can this book help?

This book is a handy toolkit filled with useful tools to help you feel better about your body. We want you to feel confident, comfortable and happy in your own skin. Here's a summary of what you will find:

→ **Quick and easy:** We've broken the book into bite-sized chunks which take only 10 minutes a day.

→ **Techniques that work:** We based this book on effective methods including cognitive behavioural therapy (CBT). CBT helps change how you think, feel and behave to overcome anxiety, sadness, shame or distress about your body or appearance.

→ **Mindfulness tools:** You will learn simple ways to pause, appreciate the moment and step back from distressing or negative thoughts and feelings.

→ **Be kinder to yourself:** You also will learn to treat yourself in more positive ways, becoming fairer and less critical of how you look. This will help you to appreciate your body and get the most out of life.

We have put this into a simple format we call 10-minute GROWTH steps. Here is a quick overview:

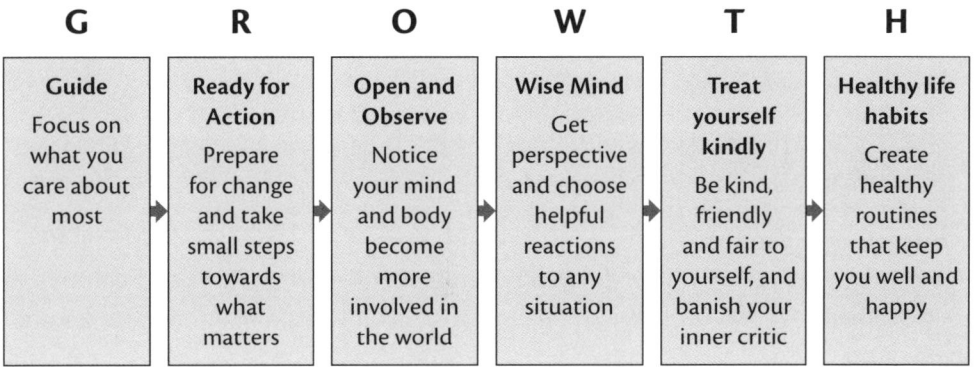

G	**R**	**O**	**W**	**T**	**H**
Guide Focus on what you care about most	**Ready for Action** Prepare for change and take small steps towards what matters	**Open and Observe** Notice your mind and body become more involved in the world	**Wise Mind** Get perspective and choose helpful reactions to any situation	**Treat yourself kindly** Be kind, friendly and fair to yourself, and banish your inner critic	**Healthy life habits** Create healthy routines that keep you well and happy

What will we cover in this book?

The book is divided into three sections:

Part 1 – Understanding Body Image: We will learn more about appearance concerns, including how they develop and some things that may keep the problem going. We will also explore how being too focused on body image can affect your feelings, thoughts and actions.

Part 2 – 10-minute GROWTH Steps to Befriend Your Body: This section will look at six key skills that can help you find more acceptance of your appearance and shift your attention to other important personal qualities and interests.

Part 3 – Making Friends with Your Body: In this section, we will help to build your confidence and stop appearance concerns from limiting how you live your life. The chapters will cover:

→ coping with strong emotions: skills to cope with intense feelings or distress

→ boosting body confidence: learning to believe in yourself and to appreciate your strengths and positive qualities

→ body confident communication: learn to tackle negative comments from others as you develop skills in communicating with confidence.

How to get the most out of this book

We have made the book as interactive as possible. Each chapter includes sections where you will be invited to:

→ **Read This:** background information and explanations to make sense of what happens when you are struggling with body image concerns and ways to overcome it.

→ **Pause and Think:** opportunities to stop and think about how things are affecting you personally.

→ **Try This:** practical ideas and activities you can carry out to practise skills in your own life.

We've also included space in the book to keep a note of your thoughts. Writing things down can help you see things differently, remember helpful insights and commit to trying something new. Look out for the footsteps icon for opportunities to try something out.

The book also includes many examples of young people who are finding ways to understand and overcome their own body image struggles. The characters are fictional, but the examples have been developed and inspired by our experiences working with real individuals over many years.

Building new habits

Change can be difficult and, at first, it might seem more comfortable to stick with what you know. This is like putting on a new pair of trainers for the first time. Even though you know your old ones are worn out and need replacing, the new trainers feel different and may even be a bit uncomfortable at first. However, after a while, they will start to feel like a good fit and you will soon become confident in your stride.

We are going to encourage you to keep practising the changes that you make until – just like the new trainers – you feel comfortable and the changes in your body image become a habit. Remember, you only have to take small steps and build your confidence gradually from each success.

 Pause and Think  5 Minutes

Are concerns about your appearance affecting your life?

Take a few minutes to think about how body and appearance concerns may be affecting your life. This can help you to understand yourself better and motivate you to get started with making a change.

How is concern or worry about your body image affecting you and your life?	
What are you missing out on? Have you stopped doing something because you have lost confidence? Are you avoiding people or places because of worries about your body or appearance?	
How would life be different or better if you were more body confident? What would you be doing differently or more of?	

Ross completed the activity. Here are his answers.

How is concern or worry about your body image affecting you and your life?	I'm constantly stressed and wondering whether everyone thinks I look skinny and weak. Sometimes it's hard to concentrate on my studies or even to focus when I'm watching my favourite YouTuber. It's really hard to stop worrying about my appearance.
What are you missing out on? Have you stopped doing something because you have lost confidence? Are you avoiding people or places because of worries about your body or appearance?	I've stopped going out with my mates in case they tease me about my size. I've also been avoiding going to the gym because I hate seeing myself in the big mirrors there and watching all the big guys working out just makes me feel really weedy in comparison.
How would life be different or better if you were more body confident? What would you be doing differently or more of?	I'd like to get back to how things used to be – I never worried about my looks and I felt fit and confident about my body. I'd like to be able to hang out with my mates without being so sensitive about what they say, maybe seeing it as a joke and giving them a hard time back. It would be good to be able to go to the gym without worrying about my appearance and get back to doing all the sports I enjoy.

Summary

→ Body image and appearance concerns are a growing problem among young people, influenced by many things including advertising and social media.

→ This book is based on effective treatments including CBT and mindfulness.

→ You will get the most out of this book if you try the exercises to find out what works best for you.

Final thoughts

Make a note of anything you have found helpful, interesting or surprising so far.

....

....

....

....

....

....

What are you going to do now? Can you choose one small action for the coming week based on what you have read so far? Can you commit to reading this book and spending time on yourself for 10 minutes each day? Anything else?

....

....

....

....

....

....

Part 1

UNDERSTANDING BODY IMAGE

Chapter 1

MAKING SENSE OF BODY IMAGE

Your body image will be shaped by many different things and can change over time. It's affected by your personal traits, like your personality and interests, as well as external influences such as society, media and those around you.

Body image problems are common and affect many young people and adults across the world. If you are struggling, remember it's not your fault and it's often due to factors beyond your control.

To improve your body image, it's helpful to understand the different factors that may affect how you see yourself. So, in this chapter, we will:

➔ explore what might be influencing how you see your body and your appearance

➔ discover which situations, people and places are most likely to trigger your body image concerns.

 Read This   🕐 10 Minutes

The impact of the media

Diya: I spend a lot of time on social media, following popular influencers and celebrities who are always promoting diets, workouts and beauty products. Every time I scroll through my feed, I see pictures of slim, toned bodies, blonde hair and perfect skin – no one looks anything like me! I constantly compare my body to theirs and think I don't measure up. When I look in the mirror, I just see a spotty face and a chubby figure. I often ask my friends if I look OK, but I find it really hard to believe them when they say something nice about my appearance.

The media will have a powerful impact on your body image. As soon as you turn on your phone, tablet or computer you'll be bombarded by ads, movies, social media and more, all showing flawless bodies based on unrealistic standards of beauty, strength or appearance. These images often show people laughing, looking relaxed or doing amazing things, linking body image with happiness, achievement or success.

Social media encourages constant comparison with others. You may find yourself comparing your own body to these impossible standards and judging yourself negatively. It's easy to develop a distorted perception about how you look and feel dissatisfied or insecure about your own body.

The media images are often biased or based on stereotypes about many important issues such as gender, disability, age, sexual orientation or race. You might start to believe that you need a certain body type or look to be accepted and valued by the world. This can negatively affect your physical and mental health, leading to self-doubt, anxiety, sadness and shame.

Remember, media images are often artificial and digitally enhanced or filtered to create a 'perfect' or idealized impression. Real bodies come in all shapes and sizes and can't be airbrushed! By recognizing this, you can start to embrace diversity and accept and appreciate your own body.

 Pause and Think **5 Minutes**

Use the following table to think about how the media affects how you see your body and appearance.

Do you think the media influences how you see yourself or others?	

Do you compare yourself to the images you see on different types of media? How does this make you feel about your own body?	
Do you think the media accurately represents the many different types of body or appearance that we see in the real world? How do you think the emphasis on certain beauty standards affects your own body image and self-esteem?	

 **Read This**  **5 Minutes**

Society and culture

Society and culture also play a part in shaping your body image. Different cultures have varying ideals of beauty, with some valuing curvier figures and others preferring slim or athletic appearances. Gender also plays a role, and can influence expectations for your weight, body shape or how muscular you are. These narrow standards often overlook or exclude young people from under-represented groups, including those defined by race, ethnicity or sexual orientation. This can lead to body dissatisfaction and insecurity amongst these young individuals.

Society often exaggerates the importance of physical appearance. Body shaming and criticism are widespread, leading to negative body image and dissatisfaction. You might start to believe that your appearance is more important than qualities such as kindness, fairness or honesty. You may also begin to believe that your value or self-worth depends on how you look.

Understanding the link between culture and body image is crucial. As individuals, if we begin to challenge society's beauty standards and embrace diversity, then we may be able to help create a more inclusive and accepting environment for everyone.

 Pause and Think  **5 Minutes**

How do you think society and culture have affected your body image? Are there any particular beauty standards or ideals that you feel pressured to live up to?	

Have you ever felt discriminated against or experienced prejudice because of your appearance or identity? This could happen face-to-face or online. Have you seen this happening to anyone else?	

 **Read This** **5 Minutes**

Peer pressure

Teenagers and young adults often feel the need to fit in with their peers, which can greatly affect body image. The desire to belong is a natural part of being human as we have always lived in groups for survival and safety. This will often include wanting to 'look the part' by having an appearance that matches those of your peers.

Worrying about not fitting in or being judged negatively by your peers can cause stress, anxiety and loss of confidence, and lead to body image concerns. You might find yourself constantly comparing yourself to those around you or feel pressured to change your appearance to be accepted or avoid negative comments.

Experiencing bullying, body shaming or negative comments about your appearance from peers can also have a huge effect on your self-image and mental health. It can lead to feelings of depression, anxiety, shame and a lack of self-esteem or confidence.

 Pause and Think **5 Minutes**

Do you feel under pressure to look a certain way to fit in or keep up with your peers?	
Have you ever been bullied or experienced negative comments about your body or appearance, either face-to-face or online?	

 **Read This** **5 Minutes**

Family values

Your family's beliefs and attitudes can greatly influence how you see yourself. If there's a strong focus on looks or appearance, or if there are frequent unkind comments or criticism about how you look, you may begin to see your body negatively. There may also be a clash of values or opinions about appropriate dress or outward appearance.

However, a supportive family that values you beyond your appearance and encourages open conversations about body image can help boost your self-acceptance and confidence.

 Pause and Think **5 Minutes**

How have your family's beliefs and values about body image affected how you see yourself?	

 **Read This** **10 Minutes**

Your body and development

> **Noah:** I really struggled when I first started to get hairs on my chin and chest. It looked so weird – like my face wasn't my own. As the oldest of my siblings, I had no idea what to expect when I became a teenager. My dad is always working and doesn't talk much, and my mum gets embarrassed and avoids talking about bodies and development. I was one of the first in my class to go through these changes, and it was so embarrassing. I felt different to everyone else, and I just wanted to fit in and for things to stay the same. I also had lots of big, angry, red spots, which made shaving difficult. My voice would drop unexpectedly, and some of my classmates would laugh so I stopped speaking up in class. Getting changed for sport became a nightmare. I tried to cover myself up and avoided PE lessons as much as possible. It was a really tough time.

Teenagers and young adults go through a period of tremendous development and change. This is linked to changing hormones, which affect your body shape, skin, height and weight. Conditions like acne can also affect how you feel about your body. It's normal to feel uncomfortable with these changes, which can occur at different times and in different ways for everyone. Living with a changing body may make you feel self-conscious or insecure, but this is part of your growth and development. Learning to accept these changes is key to a positive body image.

During this time, your brain is also developing, especially in areas that control emotions and decision-making. This can lead to strong emotions and impulsive actions. You might find it difficult to understand others' perspectives, react strongly to disagreements or feel especially sensitive to being excluded or teased by friends or peers. These brain changes can also influence how you feel about your body.

Specific challenges

Physical health conditions or disabilities can affect how your body looks and functions and may influence your self-image. Certain medications or treatments can affect your appearance or weight. Mental health problems such as anxiety, depression or eating disorders can also contribute to body image problems.

Body image concerns may also arise in young people with neurodivergence such as autism, ADHD or dyslexia. The pressure to fit in and meet societal beauty standards can be especially challenging for neurodivergent individuals who may already feel different or struggle with acceptance from peers or with social interactions. You may start comparing yourself to others or see yourself in negative ways. Sensory processing differences can also cause discomfort or distress with certain clothing styles, materials, textures or physical sensations, making it more challenging to conform to societal expectations about appearance.

Gender dysphoria occurs when there is a disconnect between your assigned gender at birth and your gender identity. While body image concerns can be present in people with gender dysphoria, it is important to recognize that this is a separate experience related to gender identity rather than body image. We do not have the scope to cover gender dysphoria in this book but have included some useful resources in our support section at the back of the book.

 **Pause and Think**  **5 Minutes**

How have any physical changes and growth affected how you see yourself or your body image?	
What else has affected your body image? For example, are you living with physical health challenges, disability or neurodivergence?	

 **Read This**  **10 Minutes**

Your personality and interests

Some personality types may make you more at risk of body image concerns. If you are introverted or shy then you may be more likely to compare yourself negatively to others, especially in social situations. You might also be more self-conscious about how you look and experience anxiety if you feel scrutinized or judged by others.

Being a perfectionist can also contribute to body image concerns, as you may tend to set unrealistic expectations for your appearance and strive for an idealized version of yourself. This can lead to negative feelings if you feel you are not meeting these high standards.

Certain interests or hobbies can increase the focus on your body image. Activities like gymnastics, dance, bodybuilding and modelling place a strong emphasis on your physical body or appearance. These hobbies are often positive and healthy, but, if taken to extremes, the culture and expectations around them may create pressure to maintain a certain weight or body shape which can lead to body dissatisfaction and unhealthy behaviours.

Developing self-confidence, self-acceptance and beliefs in your own self-worth can positively impact how you see your body. Engaging in activities or hobbies that focus on skills, talents or personal achievements can help build your self-esteem and self-worth, and help you place less emphasis on your body and appearance. We will discuss this more in later chapters.

Noah: It's been helpful to realize that many things can affect how I see my body. I'm quite shy, which makes it hard for me to talk to friends or teachers about my worries. I'm also a bit of a perfectionist and I always want to get things right. I realized that I've been feeling the same way about my body – wanting to look a certain way even though it's changing in ways I can't control. It's scary but also reassuring to know that these changes aren't my fault and that everyone goes through them at some point.

 Pause and Think 10 Minutes

What situations trigger your body image concerns?

Even if some things that affect how you feel about your body are hard to change, it's useful to pay attention to patterns or personal triggers for those feelings. You may be able to notice situations or specific people that make you more likely to feel insecure or negative about your appearance. Understanding these triggers can help you to find better ways to cope.

Now, look at the checklist below and make a note of which situations tend to make you feel insecure, uncertain or experience negative thoughts and feelings about your body or appearance.

Situation	Would this trigger body image concerns or distress? What examples can you think of?
Sports or activities that emphasize physical appearance such as going to the gym or fitness classes	
Social events or parties where you feel aware of your appearance	
Trying on clothes in a fitting room or shopping for new clothes	
Going online and seeing videos or images of celebrities or social media influencers with particular body types	

Going to a swimming pool or to the beach where there may be pressure to wear revealing swimwear	
Activities that involve physical contact or intimacy such as dating or close relationships	
Looking in the mirror or seeing your reflection when you are out and about	
Taking selfies or posting photos of yourself online	
Hanging out with certain friends who make negative comments or are very focused on body image	
Receiving comments or criticism about your appearance from family, friends or even strangers	
Having to wear a uniform at school or particular clothes for occasions	

Diya says: Lots of these situations are really triggering for me. I was surprised to realize how many areas of my life have been affected. I avoid going clothes shopping because of the huge mirrors, and I worry that people will stare and notice how awful I look. I also avoid doing anything where I might have to show off my body too much, like going to the gym, doing exercise classes or swimming. I've even stopped going out with friends because I never feel like I look as good as everyone else. My mum takes lots of care with her make-up and appearance and often points out when I'm not looking my best. This makes me tense and anxious at home because her little comments make me feel really bad.

What next?

So far, we have explored how life events, experiences and social pressures can impact how you feel about your body. While we can work together as a society to improve some of these pressures, some things might change slowly or seem beyond your control.

But here's the good news: you can pay attention to your thoughts and actions when you feel distressed about your body image. You have control over this, and understanding what's happening in your mind and body can help you to react in more helpful ways. In the next few chapters, we'll look more at how your thoughts and actions influence your emotions and body confidence.

Summary: making sense of body image

→ Concerns about body image are common and can affect anyone.

→ They can be influenced by many different factors including the media, wider society, peers, family and by your own development, personality, interests and hobbies.

→ Understanding which situations often trigger body image concerns can help you plan to react in more helpful ways.

Final thoughts

Make a note of anything you have found helpful, interesting or surprising from this chapter.

....

....

....

....

....

What are you going to do now? Can you choose one small action based on what you have discovered?

....

....

....

....

....

Chapter 2

THE IMPACT OF BODY IMAGE CONCERNS

Charlotte: Whenever I look in the mirror, I always feel upset and ashamed. All I can see are flaws and imperfections. I obsess over every blemish, extra pound in weight and everything that I dislike about my appearance. It's like a constant loop of distress and embarrassment playing in my mind. I get this heavy feeling in my chest and a sick feeling in my stomach. I wish I could feel better about myself but it's so hard.

Struggling with a negative body image can trigger many different emotions, including making you feel low, anxious, angry, embarrassed and ashamed. Concerns about your body image can also affect how you feel physically and alter how you live your life.

It can feel lonely and sometimes overwhelming if you are not sure how to make sense of what you are feeling or how to deal with these complicated and powerful emotions. In this chapter, we will:

→ discover how body image concerns can affect your feelings and emotions and can also cause physical sensations in your body

→ explore how body image concerns can have an impact on how you live your life.

Pause and Think  **10 Minutes**

First impressions of your body image

 Imagine you are meeting someone you have never met before at a train station. There will be lots of people around, so you need to describe your appearance in enough detail so they can recognize you easily and pick you out from the crowd.

How would you describe yourself? Write it down here:

Now read your description aloud and then answer the following questions:

What emotions did you feel when you read the description?	
How did you feel in your body? Were there any sensations? Did your posture change?	
What language did you use to describe your appearance? Did you use mostly factual descriptions, such as height, weight, hair, skin colour and what you are wearing? Were there lots of negative judgements and harsh comments?	
Did you include things you like or only those things you do not like about yourself?	

 **Read This**  **10 Minutes**

How important is your body image?

How did you find the activity above? Were you able to give a fair and balanced description of your appearance or did you find yourself focusing on flaws and things you don't like about your body? Did thinking about your appearance make you feel fed up, anxious, stressed or uncomfortable?

It's important to take good care of your body and appearance and to find a unique personal style that you are proud of. However, if you are struggling with body image, whenever you think about your appearance or do something to take care of your body, you might find yourself criticizing, blaming or shaming yourself for how you look instead of accepting and feeling proud of who you are. You might overlook all the positive aspects of your appearance and ignore your inner strengths, traits and good qualities. This can lead to an unbalanced perspective of yourself and a spiral of negative thoughts and emotions.

A big part of the problem comes from putting too much emphasis or importance on your body or appearance, or caring too much about how you look. Instead of seeing it as just one small part of what makes you unique and interesting, you might start to believe that your appearance is essential to your self-worth and feeling OK as a person. If this happens, your appearance concerns will often grow stronger and start to have a bigger impact on your mood, emotions and other areas of your life.

In the rest of this chapter, we will discover how focusing too much on your appearance can affect how you feel and live your life. Later in the book, we will also look at the many other things that make you unique and interesting apart from your looks or body. This can help reduce the amount of time you spend thinking and worrying about your appearance.

 Pause and Think **5 Minutes**

How important is body image or your appearance to you?	
How much time or energy do you spend thinking or worrying about how you look?	

 **Read This** **10 Minutes**

Making sense of different feelings

As we learned from the activity above, thinking about your body can trigger a wide range of different emotions, which can feel distressing and difficult. However, learning to recognize and name the different feelings that show up can make them feel less confusing or overwhelming.

Here are some of the common negative feelings that you might notice if you are struggling with your body image, and how they might affect you:

Negative feelings	How could this feeling affect you?
Sad, low, fed up or depressed	You can start seeing everything gloomily or negatively. You become very critical of yourself, your body and how you look. You may feel exhausted, and it might affect your sleep. You might lose motivation or interest in doing activities you used to enjoy, like spending time with friends and family or doing hobbies.
Anxious, fearful, worried or panicky	You might spend a lot of time worrying about how you look and think about scary or upsetting situations, such as imagining people teasing or laughing at you. This can make you feel stressed, anxious and fearful. Physically, you might become tense and shaky or have a racing heart, sweaty palms or a dry mouth. You might avoid situations that you think will make you feel bad about your appearance, or constantly seek reassurance from others.
Embarrassed, guilty or ashamed	You might start to blame yourself for how you look or use unkind words or body-shaming language to describe yourself. Physically, you might notice blushing, tense muscles, a hot face or a burning feeling in your chest or stomach. You might react by isolating yourself, trying to hide or cover up parts of your body, or putting immense effort into achieving the 'perfect' body. Alternatively, you might give up, telling yourself there's no point in trying as you can never achieve the body that you want.
Angry, frustrated, irritated or annoyed	You might get snappy, argumentative or irritable with friends and family, and react angrily or defensively to any comments about your body or appearance. Physically, you might feel tense and restless, with a hot face and clenched fists.

 Pause and Think   5 Minutes

Which emotions are linked to your body image?

Look at this list of distressing feelings and emotions that might be triggered by concerns about your body or appearance. Place a tick next to any you recognize and give some recent examples of when you felt this way and how the emotion affected you.

Uncomfortable feelings or emotions	Do you feel this way when thinking about your body or appearance?	What examples can you think of? How did this emotion affect you?
Sad, low, fed up or depressed		

Anxious, fearful, worried or panicky		
Embarrassed, guilty or ashamed		
Angry, frustrated, irritated or annoyed		

If low mood or anxiety are bigger problems that affect areas of your life other than your body image, then you may also wish to take a look at the other books in this series:

10 Minutes to Beat Anxiety and Panic: A Step-by-Step Guide for Teens Using CBT and Mindfulness

10 Minutes to Boost Your Mood: A Step-by-Step Guide for Teens Using CBT and Mindfulness

Seek help if you are struggling

If you are having strong or distressing emotions, especially if you are feeling low, fed up or hopeless, then you may sometimes have thoughts about harming yourself or about death or suicide. If this is true for you, please talk to a trusted adult or seek help from your doctor. You could also call, message or email a support organization such as Childline or the Samaritans.

We talk more about coping with strong or distressing emotions in Chapter 14 and there are links to support organizations at the back of this book.

 **Pause and Think**  **5 Minutes**

Changes in your body

Living with concerns or focus on body image can cause many body sensations and symptoms. These can be uncomfortable and unpleasant but are not harmful and will usually pass once the emotion settles down.

Look at this checklist of physical changes that you might notice if your mood or emotions are being affected by appearance concerns:

Over the past 2 weeks, have you been affected often or very often by the following body changes?	Tick if you have noticed this.
Trouble getting to sleep or waking in the night	
Having less energy and feeling exhausted	
Finding it hard to concentrate on watching TV, reading or other activities	
Aches and pains, including headaches and muscle aches, or prickly or tingling sensations	
Physical feelings of anxiety such as a racing heart or a tight chest, feeling shaky, sweaty, or restless and agitated	
Feeling slowed down	
Feeling jumpy, fidgety or easily startled	
Headaches or migraines	
Butterflies, stomach pains, bloating or feeling sick	
Feeling light-headed, faint or dizzy	

Charlotte says: I have a lot of negative feelings about my body. I ticked all four boxes in the emotions chart! These emotions can be quite overwhelming, so I found it helpful to have a list and give a name to how I was feeling. Sometimes I feel sad and fed up, and other times I'm tense and anxious. I often feel embarrassed and ashamed of how I look. And I definitely get angry and defensive whenever my parents or friends try to talk to me about it. I also get lots of sensations in my body. I get tense in my arms, my face feels hot and I have a churning feeling in my gut, which is quite uncomfortable. It has helped me to know that these sensations are due to my emotions and that they will go away once I start to feel better.

 Read This  10 Minutes

Does body image affect how you live your life?

We have explored how concerns about your body image can affect your emotions and cause physical sensations in your body. Now we will think about how appearance concerns can affect you in other ways. Let's look at some of the different parts of your life that might be affected.

Relationships with friends and family

Worrying about how you look can affect your relationships. If you are concerned that others may judge you negatively, you might avoid social events or close relationships. Even when you do go out, you may be so caught up in worrying about your appearance that it's hard to relax and enjoy yourself.

Your friends and family may find it hard to understand how you are feeling as they may see you very differently from how you see yourself. They could get frustrated if you frequently talk about your appearance or ask for reassurance, and they may get upset if there doesn't seem to be an easy solution to help you feel better. This can all lead to missing out on opportunities to connect with people that are important to you.

School and studies

If you spend a lot of time and effort worrying about how you look or carrying out lengthy beauty, cosmetics or exercise regimes, it can interfere with other important activities like studying. You might skip or avoid classes or attend school less often because you are worried about what others think of your appearance. Concerns about body image can also be distracting and make it hard to concentrate or focus, which could negatively impact your grades and overall achievement.

Hobbies and fun

Feeling fed up, low, anxious, embarrassed and ashamed due to body image concerns can lead you to cut down on many activities that you used to enjoy like sports, hobbies and other fun experiences. This means that you miss out on many opportunities to relax, have fun and enjoy yourself. Life can start feeling flat and dull, with fewer chances to feel enthusiastic, upbeat, motivated or happy.

Physical health

Concerns about your appearance can also lead to behaviours that are potentially harmful to your physical wellbeing, such as excessive dieting, over-exercising, taking muscle-building supplements or developing unhealthy eating habits. If you recognize any of these behaviours, you may have developed an eating disorder, or your health may be at risk, and we strongly recommend that you see your doctor for a physical health check and further support and advice.

Work and finances

Sometimes concerns about body image mean that you get drawn into spending a lot of money on products such as cosmetics or clothing, or even on treatments or procedures to try and improve or change your appearance in some way. Feeling anxious, low or embarrassed may also make it difficult to go to work at all. You might avoid public-facing jobs or activities because you don't want to be exposed to possible attention, criticism or scrutiny by others.

 Pause and Think **10 Minutes**

Make a note in the table below about how concerns about body image affect the different areas of your life.

Area of your life	Is this area of your life affected by concerns about body image? Give some examples.
Relationships with friends and family	
School and studies	
Hobbies and fun	
Physical health	
Work and finances	

Charlotte says: My life is being affected in many ways. I keep arguing with my mum and sister because they always say I look nice, but I never believe them. They care about me a lot, but I think they're fed up with me constantly complaining about how bad I look. It's hard to concentrate on studying at home because I keep getting up to check or fix my hair and make-up in the mirror or I end up looking on social media for ideas to improve my appearance. I feel bad about how much time this takes, but it's hard to motivate myself to concentrate on schoolwork. I don't have much money, but I spend everything I can on cosmetics and beauty products – but they are so expensive! I wish I had more money, but I don't have the confidence to try to get a part-time job.

 **Try This** **2 Minutes**

Notice the NOW to cope with difficult feelings

We will learn lots of skills for coping with difficult emotions as we continue through this book. For the moment, try this simple and quick technique to help you cope with any strong or difficult emotion that's being triggered by concerns about your body image. There are three steps:

1. **N**otice and name your thoughts and feelings: I'm worrying about the spot on my face. I'm anxious about having to talk in front of the class tomorrow. I'm thinking about how big my bum looks in these jeans. I feel embarrassed and stressed. My stomach is churning and my face is hot. My hands are shaking.

2. **O**bserve sensations outside your body and the world around you: I'm sitting on my bed and I can feel the soft mattress underneath me. I can feel my feet on the floor. I can wriggle my toes and stretch my arms up above my head. I can see a blue water bottle and a purple book on the table. I can hear traffic outside my window.

3. **W**hat matters? Decide what's most important for you to focus on and then move on to do this with your full attention. I've got to finish this essay by tomorrow. I want to enjoy the programme I'm watching on TV. I want to enjoy chatting with my friend and listening to what she's saying because she's telling a funny story.

 Pause and Think  **10 Minutes**

Developing more positive emotions

As we progress through this book, we will explore ways to turn down the volume of negative emotions and become more aware of more positive emotions concerning your body image. This could include feeling:

➜ happy, content, cheerful, joyful

➜ peaceful, relaxed, calm and at ease

➜ confident, proud, motivated, strong, accomplished

➜ excited, enthusiastic, energetic

➜ accepted, liberated, grateful, free.

Look through the list of positive emotions above and then answer these questions.

Which of these emotions would you like to feel more of about your body image?	
Choose one of these positive emotions. How would you behave differently if you felt more like this? What difference would it make in your day-to-day life?	
Can you make any tiny changes by behaving 'as if' you felt more like this?	

Summary: the impact of body image concerns

➜ Concerns about your appearance and body image can cause many emotions, including feeling sad, low, anxious, embarrassed, ashamed and angry.

➜ These feelings can cause physical reactions in your body, such as tiredness, poor sleep, shaking, sweating, restlessness and aches and pains.

➜ Body image concerns can affect many areas of life, including your relationships, school, hobbies, health and finances.

➜ Putting too much focus or importance on body image can affect your confidence and self-esteem.

Final thoughts

Make a note of anything you have found helpful, interesting or surprising from this chapter.

....

....

....

....

....

....

What are you going to do now? Can you choose one small action based on what you have discovered?

....

....

....

....

....

....

Chapter 3

BODY IMAGE AND YOUR MIND

Vihaan: I get really stressed before I go out with my friends. A lot of them are really fashion conscious and always have the latest trainers and cool hairstyles. They always look good, even if we're just hanging out at the park. I never feel I look right, and my dad can't afford to buy the brands that everyone wears. I always feel like I'm boring and geeky next to them. I also have acne which causes spots on my face and back. I'm on treatment but I worry that it makes me stand out and look even worse. I keep thinking that everyone will laugh at me, or that they wouldn't want me to be part of the group anymore. Sometimes I get so worked up that I don't bother to go out at all.

Your mind is an incredible and powerful tool. It allows you to problem-solve, to be amazingly creative and to imagine wonderful possibilities. Being able to think, work things out, plan and communicate makes you unique and human. However, your mind is not always your friend, and the things you imagine, the way you see yourself and the conclusions you jump to may not always be accurate or helpful for building your confidence and self-esteem.

Your thoughts and mindset can have a big impact on how you feel and what you do. Spending a lot of time thinking negatively about how you look can take up a lot of time and energy, making you feel fed up, anxious and low. In this chapter, we will:

→ discover how your thoughts about your body and appearance can affect your feelings and self-confidence

→ learn to spot when negative thoughts about your body show up without giving them too much attention or allowing them to influence your actions

→ uncover your personal 'Body Bullies' – unhelpful thoughts about your appearance that can show up in your mind and crush your body confidence.

Pause and Think 5 Minutes

How does body image affect your thoughts and beliefs about yourself?

We all have occasional negative thoughts or worries about how we look. But when these thoughts happen frequently, they can become a pattern. Answering these questions will help you discover any unhelpful thinking habits related to body image that may be affecting your confidence and mood.

Thoughts about your body or appearance	Do you think this way often or very often (yes/no)?
Do you often put yourself down, criticize or negatively judge your body or appearance?	
Do you spend more time thinking about things that you don't like about how you look rather than things that you like or are proud of?	
Do you believe that your body is unattractive or ugly in some way?	
Do you worry that others will judge you negatively based on your appearance?	
Does thinking or worrying about your appearance stop you from doing important things like studying, seeing friends or doing hobbies?	
Do you believe that your body or appearance defines your importance or self-worth?	
Do you blame your appearance for any feelings of unhappiness or dissatisfaction in your life?	

If you have answered yes to three or more of these questions, then read on! This chapter will start to help you understand more about the links between thoughts about your body image and your emotions and confidence.

 Read This 10 Minutes

The power of your mind

Thoughts are the words and pictures that flow constantly through your mind that help you make sense of the world and express your feelings, wishes and ideas. They include plans, ideas, hopes, dreams, stories, images, fears, worries and memories, both good and bad.

Your thoughts can be about anything and everything in the present, past or future! They might be about things that make you happy, things that are neutral or things that you dislike or fear. They can make you feel distressed, pleased, amused or uncomfortable.

Your mind is very active with many thoughts passing through it each day. Some of these are automatic and will pop into your mind uninvited, often about routine or everyday things, like which cereal to pick for breakfast. These typically pass through your mind mostly unnoticed.

Thoughts can be more powerful if you give them your full attention and believe them as the absolute truth, especially when they come with strong feelings like sadness, anger or anxiety. These feelings can be triggered by upsetting thoughts about your body or appearance.

But even if they *feel* true, your thoughts may not be correct or accurate. You don't have to take your thoughts too seriously, especially if they are negative or causing you distress. It can help to remind yourself that your thoughts are not facts. They are just ideas, guesses, possibilities or opinions and they can change depending on the day or situation.

Recognizing unhelpful thoughts and treating them as opinions rather than facts is an important first step. It can also help to step back from thoughts and not get so caught up by them, especially the unhelpful ones that seem to play over and over. Instead, try to see them as 'just another thought'. As we continue through this book, we will discover lots of different skills in how to do this.

 **Read This** **10 Minutes**

Watching a movie in your mind

Imagine that your mind is a movie theatre, and your thoughts are the different films shown throughout the day. Some might be happy and upbeat, some relaxing or amusing, while others could be sad, exciting or scary.

The movie is not happening in real life, it's just playing in your mind, but your body and emotions can still react very strongly. Your imagination can generate images and stories that feel convincing and realistic. So, as you watch the movie, you might feel emotions such as excitement or fear, with physical reactions like a racing heart or sweaty palms when the hero is in danger.

Different films will affect you in different ways. If your mind plays dark and gloomy movies, you might start to feel depressed or low. Watching scary movies full of horror or suspense can make you feel anxious, tense and jumpy, leaving you on edge long after the movie has finished. On the other hand, watching an upbeat or inspiring movie about overcoming challenges and following your dreams can make you feel more confident and ready to face your problems.

It's easy to get so absorbed by a movie that you feel trapped in your seat unable to find the exit, even if it is a scary or upsetting story. As we continue through this book, we will learn ways to step outside the movie theatre and choose to watch something more enjoyable or motivating. You will also discover how to shrink down the movie screen to the size of your phone screen. Even if the movie is still playing, it's now much smaller and quieter, so you can put it in your pocket and get on with your day.

 Pause and Think   **10 Minutes**

What movie starts playing when you think about your body or your appearance? Is it a light-hearted comedy? A dark or gloomy drama? Or a scary movie filled with danger and terrifying possibilities around every corner?	
Do you ever get trapped in the movie theatre watching the same story about your body over and over? How does this feel? What are you missing out on because you are watching this film on repeat?	

 **Read This**   **10 Minutes**

Thoughts about your body

Your thoughts about your body or appearance can be positive or negative, helpful or unhelpful, or a mixture of all of these. Looking in the mirror at your hair one morning, you might think 'I have curly black hair'. This is a neutral thought that simply describes your hair. Another thought could be: 'My hair looks great today!' This is a positive thought that might make you feel happy or proud. Or you might think: 'I hate my hair, it always looks so messy'. This is a more negative thought that could make you feel fed up or worried.

When you are struggling with concerns about your appearance, then there will be very few neutral or positive thoughts about your body. Instead, your thoughts will be like watching a horror movie that leaves you feeling fed up, anxious, stressed and embarrassed. This movie is extremely absorbing and you quickly get trapped thinking about your body and appearance in negative ways. You might find yourself:

→ constantly on the lookout for negative comments or criticisms while ignoring or discounting any compliments or nice things that people say

→ worrying obsessively about your appearance and thinking it should be flawless

→ magnifying small imperfections out of proportion, seeing them as bad or defective rather than interesting, different and unique to you

→ constantly comparing yourself negatively with your peers or friendship group.

This unpleasant movie can get stuck on a loop, with upsetting words or images showing up over and over in your mind, such as:

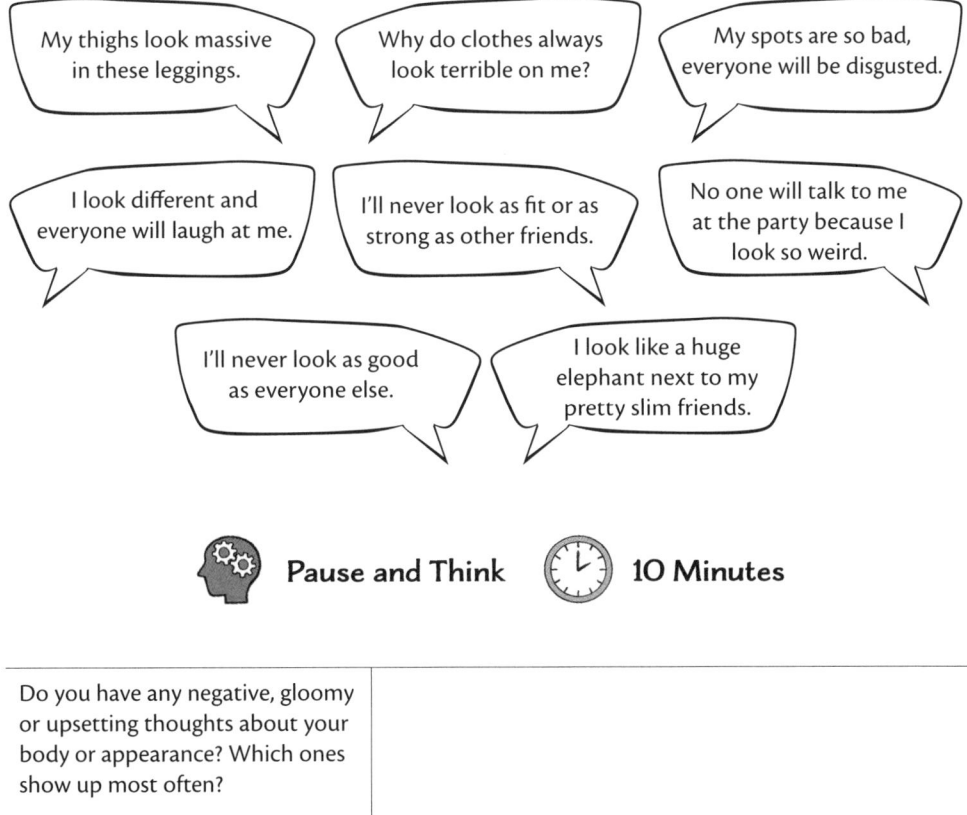

My thighs look massive in these leggings.

Why do clothes always look terrible on me?

My spots are so bad, everyone will be disgusted.

I look different and everyone will laugh at me.

I'll never look as fit or as strong as other friends.

No one will talk to me at the party because I look so weird.

I'll never look as good as everyone else.

I look like a huge elephant next to my pretty slim friends.

Pause and Think **10 Minutes**

Do you have any negative, gloomy or upsetting thoughts about your body or appearance? Which ones show up most often?	
Do these thoughts usually show up as words or as pictures in your mind? What examples can you think of?	

How do these thoughts make you feel? How do they affect your confidence?	
How do these thoughts affect your actions and how you live your life? Do they stop you from doing anything important or fun?	

Vihaan completed this activity.

Do you have any negative thoughts about your body or appearance? Which ones show up most often? Which ones are the most upsetting?	I often think that I look boring and I'm not wearing the right clothes. The most difficult thoughts are about how bad I look compared to others in my friend group, and when I imagine myself being laughed at by everyone.
Do these thoughts usually show up as words or as pictures in your mind? What examples can you think of?	I get words such as 'you look like a loser' and 'you are such a geek'. I also get a picture in my head about what I must look like to others. It's usually me looking boring and stupid and with spotty skin, next to everyone else looking cool in designer gear.
How do these thoughts make you feel? How do they affect your confidence?	When I start worrying about how I look, I feel very anxious and I lose loads of confidence. I get shaky hands and I start sweating when I even think about hanging out with that group.
How do these thoughts affect your actions and how you live your life? Do they stop you from doing anything important or fun?	I've stopped seeing a lot of friends, even people who are less focused on fashion, because I worry that I don't look good enough. I've stopped going to the gym, and I don't play football much anymore now. I'm feeling really isolated and fed up.

 **Read This**  **5 Minutes**

Meet the Body Bullies

One way to make negative thoughts seem less distressing and more manageable is to see them as speech bubbles coming from an imaginary character. This helps you to recognize them as unhelpful thoughts, not facts.

The 'Body Bullies' are patterns of negative thoughts, beliefs and opinions about your appearance that have become stuck and hard to ignore. They constantly remind you about everything you dislike about your appearance, often using very harsh and mean words.

The Body Bullies are usually very talkative – but only about one thing – *your appearance*! They tend to:

→ **talk endlessly about how bad you look,** bringing negative thoughts into your mind over and over again

→ **point out everything that you dislike about your appearance** while ignoring everything positive

→ **criticize, judge and blame you for not looking a certain way** even if this is based on images that are airbrushed or unrealistic

→ **insist that your looks are the only thing that matters,** ignoring all your other abilities, strengths and good qualities

→ **call you unkind names** based on your body or appearance.

The Body Bullies aren't accurate, helpful or truthful, but their messages may feel familiar and believable because they've been around for a while. Even though they shouldn't be trusted, they can seem very convincing and can make you feel fed up, embarrassed and anxious because of the harsh things they say.

The Body Bullies are like unwanted party spoilers coming into your mind and causing disruption. They spoil your fun, crush your confidence and make you feel anxious and down. They can also keep you trapped and stop you from doing things you enjoy that matter to you.

Here are some of the common Body Bullies. Do you recognize any of these?

Attention Grabber
'Appearance is everything'
Demands high standards
Relentless and bossy

Gloomy Gaze
Only notices negative
comments or problems with
your appearance and ignores
compliments

Over Thinker
Unable to stop worrying about
how you look, always exaggerating
the risks of not looking right and
expecting the worst

Cruel Critic
Gives you a hard time and
calls you mean names if
you don't look right

Self-Scrutinizer
Constantly looking for problems in every
detail of your appearance and compares
you negatively to everyone else

Pause and Think   **10 Minutes**

Spotting the Body Bullies

Use this table to think about which Body Bullies most often show up in your mind, and how you react when they appear.

Which Body Bullies show up most in your mind? Is it just one or two, or do they appear together as a group?	
Create an image for each Body Bully. What do they look like? Can you see them as animated characters or silly creatures? Can you find a way for them to be light-hearted or funny rather than serious and scary?	
What do they sound like? Give each character a voice that suits them best. Do they sound squeaky, deep, hoarse, croaky or shouty?	

What does each Body Bully say? What do they focus on? How powerful or loud are their voices? Can you call them out or does what they say seem believable?	
How do you feel when the Body Bullies appear? What happens to your mood or emotions? How do they affect your confidence or motivation?	
How do the Body Bullies affect your life? Are they changing what you do or how you spend your time? What are you missing out on because of these Body Bullies and their negative messages?	

Vihaan says: I can recognize nearly all the Body Bullies! Attention Grabber is especially loud and strong. It makes me focus on my appearance a lot of the time instead of thinking about my fitness and my friendships. I don't want that! I also relate to Self-Scrutinizer. I'm constantly looking at myself and noticing every small thing that's wrong with my appearance. Then I compare myself to the other boys and I always feel much worse. Although I still worry a lot about how I look, using the Body Bullies is a fun way of thinking about what's happening and helps make my negative thoughts seem less powerful. I can call those Body Bullies out! I'm looking forward to finding out the best way to deal with them.

 **Read This** ⏱ **5 Minutes**

Where do the Body Bullies come from?

Your personal Body Bullies develop for many reasons, including the impact of society, social media, life events, people around you and your personality – all the things that we explored in Chapter 1.

Imagine these Body Bullies as an inner alarm system. They want you to look your best and to fit in. However, their approach is extremely negative! Their constant threats, criticism and dire predictions often crush your confidence and leave you feeling stressed, upset and anxious.

 **Try This**   **10 Minutes**

Call out your Body Bullies by NAME

As with most bullies in life, Body Bullies can be difficult to deal with. If you listen to them and believe everything they say, then you can lose confidence and stop doing many enjoyable and important things.

We will explore many ways to become 'bully-proof' as we carry on through this book. The first step is to recognize that they have shown up and to start calling them out. This will stop you from getting so caught up, pushed around and bothered by what they are telling you.

To make a start, can you try giving each Body Bully a **NAME**? This is a four-step approach to notice that the Body Bullies have shown up and that they are trying to push you around or give you a hard time:

→ **N**otice that you have started to feel anxious, down or lacking in confidence. Try saying: 'I'm having some uncomfortable thoughts and feelings right now. My chest is tight, my heart is thumping and I feel a bit sick.'

→ **A**cknowledge the Body Bullies have shown up and greet them by name. Say: 'Hi Attention Grabber, hello Self-Scrutinizer! I know you both really well. Welcome to the party!'

→ **M**ake friends with the Body Bullies – there's no need to fight them, argue with them or try to get rid of them. Just accept that they have shown up and that they have a lot to say, but you don't have to believe every word!

→ **E**xpand your attention. Don't let the Body Bullies dominate! What else is in the room or around you that is interesting? Notice three things you can see, three things you can hear and three things you can touch. This can help shift your attention and get things in more perspective so they are less able to affect you or boss you around. Finish by thinking about what's most important to do next and try to do this with as much attention as you can.

Summary: body image and your mind

→ Your thoughts about your appearance can affect your feelings and confidence.

→ Even if they *feel* true, these thoughts may not be correct or accurate and can lead to you feeling stressed, fed up and embarrassed.

→ Body Bullies are patterns of negative thoughts about your appearance that have become stuck and are hard to ignore.

→ Thoughts are not facts: you don't need to believe everything that the Body Bullies say – instead, you can call them out by giving them a **NAME**.

Final thoughts

Make a note of anything you have found helpful, interesting or surprising from this chapter.

....
....
....
....
....
....

What are you going to do now? Can you choose one small action based on what you have discovered?

....
....
....
....
....
....

Chapter 4

BODY IMAGE AND YOUR ACTIONS

Asha: I spend hours on my hair, curling it, straightening it, dying it different colours and constantly checking it in the mirror. But then I always end up washing it out and starting over because it never looks exactly right. I keep thinking my face has a weird shape and that my forehead is huge so I'm always trying to cover it up. My mum gets annoyed because I'm constantly fussing with my hair instead of listening to her. I often ask my best friend if I look OK, and she always says I do, but I feel like she's just being nice. I used to do a lot of outdoor activities like hiking and rock climbing, but I've stopped because I'm worried that the wind will mess up my hair and people will be able to see how bad my face looks. I've started wearing a beanie hat all the time, even indoors, to cover my forehead. But now that it's summer, I feel hot and sweaty, and I must look silly. It's making me feel even worse!

Has body image affected how you live your life?

How you view yourself can have a big impact on your actions and how you live your life. Do you constantly check your appearance in mirrors or compare yourself to others on social media? Do you often ask for reassurance from friends and family but find it hard to believe them when they say you look OK? Are you avoiding activities you used to enjoy because of concerns about your appearance? Do you spend a lot of time trying to hide or change how you look?

Most people's actions follow repeated patterns or habits. You might not be aware of how often you are carrying out actions related to body image or the impact they have on your thoughts or emotions. However, as you learn to notice these actions, you can start making small changes that free you from unhelpful actions that have become time-consuming and costly, and get in the way of doing enjoyable things. In this chapter, we will:

→ explore actions that you might take when you are feeling worried, low or lacking body confidence

→ learn to notice your actions, even if they have become automatic habits

→ discover the impact of body image actions on your confidence, mood and enjoyment of life.

 **Read This** **5 Minutes**

What are actions?

An action is something that you do or a way you behave in a situation. Most actions can be seen by others – making a drink, studying, going for a walk and talking with friends are all types of actions. Equally, *not* doing things also involves actions. For example, if you turn down an invitation to meet friends, what are you doing instead? Are you carrying out 'Appearance Actions' such as checking yourself in the mirror or scrolling through social media and comparing yourself to online images?

Your actions can be influenced by your thoughts and your emotions. When you feel contented or happy, your actions will often involve doing things you enjoy, such as meeting friends, being active or doing work or study. If you feel down about your appearance you might withdraw from people, cover up parts of your body or avoid activities that you previously enjoyed.

 **Pause and Think** **10 Minutes**

Start to notice your actions

Think of a recent situation where you felt worried, low or anxious about your body or appearance. Now answer the following questions.

What was the situation? Where were you? Who were you with? What were you doing?	

How did you feel? What emotions did you have?	
What were you thinking? Did any of the Body Bullies show up? What were they saying?	
What were your actions in this situation? What did you do, or want to do? Did you change the choices you made or how you interacted with others?	
What was the impact of these actions? How did they help? Could there be any negative or unhelpful consequences of these actions, either straightaway or later?	

 **Read This**  **5 Minutes**

Thoughts and actions

Mental actions take place inside your mind. These can't be seen by other people but can still have a big impact. Mental actions usually involve thinking about something repeatedly, like going over embarrassing memories or worrying about future problems.

Other people cannot see your thoughts or know what is going on inside your mind. But they will be able to notice your reactions to these thoughts, such as if you have begun staring into space and have stopped listening to what they are saying because you are worrying about your body image.

Your thoughts will also influence the actions that you choose. Have your thoughts become dominated by the loud voices of the Body Bullies such as Attention Grabber and Over Thinker that we met in Chapter 3? Do you focus on all the flaws and problems with your body or constantly compare yourself negatively to others?

Spending too much time listening to the negative message of the Body Bullies can lead to actions that may be harmful in the long-term, such as avoiding important and enjoyable activities or spending a lot of time looking in mirrors as you try to check or perfect your appearance. This can take up a lot of time and energy and leave you feeling anxious, worried and low in confidence.

Pause and Think **10 Minutes**

Notice how you react to thoughts

Next, we will start to notice how you react to your thoughts. Think back to Chapter 3 – which Body Bullies most often show up in your mind when you are struggling with body image concerns? Is it Attention Grabber? Or do Self-Scrutinizer and Cruel Critic tend to visit your mind? Make a note of your most frequent Body Bullies here:

....

....

....

....

....

Now answer the following questions.

What actions do you do more often when the Body Bullies show up? Do you check or change your appearance? Do you find yourself staring into space, or is it hard to concentrate or make decisions?	
What actions do you avoid or do less often? For example, are you no longer going to places or doing certain activities? What are you doing instead?	

Asha says: Attention Grabber makes me focus a lot on my appearance, so I spend a lot of time thinking about my hair and worrying about the size of my forehead. This has stopped me from doing things that I enjoy, like being out in the fresh air and walking with friends. Cruel Critic constantly tells me how bad my hair looks, so I keep changing my hairstyle or wearing my beanie hat which makes me feel hot and self-conscious. Trying to make my hair look perfect takes a lot of time and Cruel Critic is never satisfied! Even when I get compliments,

Gloomy Gaze stops me from believing them, so I react negatively when anyone says something nice, which annoys my friends and family. I hadn't realized how many of my actions are linked to the Body Bullies and my worries about how I look.

 **Read This**  **10 Minutes**

Unhelpful Appearance Actions

It is normal and healthy to want to take care of your body. This involves many different actions like physical activity, eating well and keeping your body clean and well-cared-for. It's also important to have pride in your appearance. Maybe you want to look good at a social event, so you put on a new outfit, style your hair or add some jewellery or make-up.

However, if these actions become extreme or out of proportion, they can become a problem. If you're constantly focused on your looks or repeating appearance-related actions, they can shift from being a positive way to take care of yourself and become an unhealthy obsession.

It can be hard to notice when this has happened, especially if the Body Bullies have been around for a while and have convinced you that you must do these things to feel better about your appearance. But repeating these actions too often reinforces the false idea that your appearance is the most important thing and that you must focus on it constantly to look as good as everyone else.

We will encourage you to step back and notice *what* actions you are doing, *why* you do them, *how long* you spend on them and *how often* you do them. Ask yourself if your actions are balanced or if they are becoming extreme. You can also try to notice if these actions relieve your worries or make them worse.

In this chapter, we will explore three groups of unhelpful Appearance Actions:

→ **checking, comparing and seeking reassurance** – repeatedly checking or comparing how you look and asking others if you look OK

→ **hiding or altering your appearance** – trying to change, cover up or camouflage things you don't like about your body

→ **avoidance and seeking safety** – avoiding people, places, activities and situations that trigger negative feelings about your body image.

 **Read This**  **10 Minutes**

Comparing, checking and seeking reassurance

Appearance Actions such as checking your body, comparing yourself to others or seeking reassurance are common when you have body image concerns and can affect many parts of your life. Whether you're at the gym, or at home scrolling through social media, the urge to carry these out can be very strong, almost like a compulsion. These actions are motivated by Body Bullies like Self-Scrutinizer, who demand that you keep searching for flaws which others might criticize. They might involve looking in the mirror many times a day, touching or measuring parts of your body, or making comparisons to other people.

The urge to check or compare might provide short-term relief from appearance-related distress, but unfortunately, this doesn't last. Soon, you'll doubt your appearance again and feel the need to check once more, leading to a cycle of constant self-scrutiny. You might even find yourself examining your reflection in windows, ponds or shiny surfaces, but this won't give you an accurate or fair impression.

You might also seek frequent reassurance from others that you look OK. Kind words from friends or family may help for a while, but the positive feeling soon fades. It's also harder to accept or believe compliments because the presence of Gloomy Gaze makes you doubt or ignore them. Remember, you deserve to feel happy and confident just the way you are, not only when someone else validates your appearance!

Appearance Actions can drain your energy and distract you from school, relationships and other important life activities. So, it's important to notice and start placing limits on how much time you are spending carrying these out each day.

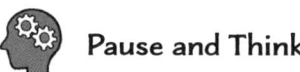 **Pause and Think**  **10 Minutes**

How often do you check, compare or seek reassurance?

Check the list of actions below and put a tick next to any that you do often or very often. Note how frequently you carry out each action in a day or week, along with the amount of time you usually spend on it. You might need to observe your behaviour for a few days to answer accurately.

Comparing, checking and reassurance-seeking actions	How often do you do this each day?	Around how many minutes do you spend on it in total?	What do you do? When and where do you do it?
Looking at your appearance in a mirror or reflective surface			
Touching, inspecting or measuring parts of your body to check how they look or feel			
Taking and looking at photos or videos to observe or monitor your body			
Comparing your appearance to people around you			
Looking at and comparing yourself to images on the internet or social media			
Talking to other people about your appearance or asking for reassurance about how you look			
Dismissing, ignoring or downplaying compliments or positive comments			
Anything else?			

 Read This  10 Minutes

Hiding or altering your appearance

When you are concerned about body image, you might also spend a lot of time trying to cover up or hide parts of your body that you consider flawed. You might wear baggy or oversized clothing to conceal your body shape or use heavy make-up to hide blemishes, scars or changes in your skin. You might style your hair to cover your face, hide behind a hat or sunglasses, or change your posture by slouching, looking downwards or putting a hand over your face. These actions are motivated by the Body Bullies who tell you that appearance is everything and that you don't look good enough.

These actions can become a problem if you overuse them or they become extreme and unhelpful. Wearing a little spot concealer or putting on make-up for a special occasion can be a way to express yourself and take pride in your appearance. However, make-up is a fun accessory, not a mask to hide behind. If your self-esteem depends on continually wearing perfect or heavy make-up, which can harm your skin and limit your life, then you may be left feeling trapped and insecure and lacking confidence in your natural appearance.

You might also try to change your body because you are not satisfied with it. You might carry out vigorous exercise or lift weights to sculpt your body shape or size, or even explore cosmetic or facial treatments, which can be expensive and sometimes harmful to your skin. Again, these actions can range from helpful self-care to becoming a major problem. Enjoying the gym or exercise is positive, but becoming obsessed with the size of your muscles, pushing yourself to extremes or taking supplements to bulk up can be a far bigger problem.

 Pause and Think  10 Minutes

How often do you try to hide or alter your appearance?

Check the list of actions below and put a tick next to any that you do often or very often. Note how frequently you carry out each action in a day or week, along with the amount of time you usually spend on it. You might need to observe your behaviour for a few days to answer accurately.

Actions to hide or alter your appearance	How often do you do this each day?	Around how many minutes do you spend on it in total?	What do you do? What areas of the body are you trying to hide or change?
Putting on or adjusting cosmetics or make-up, including skin products and concealers			
Cutting, styling, straightening and colouring your hair			
Using oversized clothing, hats, scarves etc. to hide parts of your body or shape			
Holding your body in certain postures or covering features with your hand or clothes			
Doing exercise to change your body shape or composition			
Cosmetic treatments such as facials, teeth whitening, fake tans, tattoos, hair removal and manicures			
Taking supplements to try and change your body shape			
Looking online for ways to hide or alter your appearance			
Anything else?			

Asha says: I started off washing and styling my hair before going out to parties or socializing, like most of my friends. I would check myself once in the mirror and then be ready to go and have fun! Now, I don't seem to be able to pull myself away from the mirror. I check at least ten times a day and I can stare at myself from different angles for up to 10 minutes each time. It's sometimes hard to leave the house. It means I'm always late for everything and my friends get annoyed. The more I look, the more things I find wrong, especially with my hair! I spent all my birthday money on styling brushes, hair dye and hair products and I still hate it! I can see that mirror-checking doesn't work for me!

 **Read This** **10 Minutes**

Avoidance and seeking safety

Have you started avoiding people, places or activities because of concerns about your appearance? This may happen when you fear judgement or criticism about how you look, or when something about the situation makes you more aware of aspects of your appearance that distress you.

Perhaps you avoid social situations or parties, or you cut back on going to the gym with its big mirrors and bright lights. You might stop going to exercise classes or swimming where you need to wear tight or revealing clothing. On the other hand, you might avoid photos or selfies and refuse to post images of yourself on social media for fear of negative comments or comparisons.

You might also carry out actions to try and make yourself feel safer or less at risk of scrutiny or criticism. This might involve choosing clothing or hairstyles that make you stand out less, avoiding eye contact with others, waiting until it's dark before going out or only socializing with a small group of trusted friends to reduce judgement. It can also involve editing images on social networking sites and deleting or un-tagging images you think are unflattering.

While avoiding scary or stressful situations may seem helpful in controlling feelings of anxiety or embarrassment, it can become a problem if you are repeating it:

→ **The relief is short-lived!** The unpleasant feelings will soon return, often even stronger than before.

→ **Loss of confidence and isolation.** When you avoid situations due to fear or anxiety, it becomes even harder to participate next time. You lose confidence in yourself and your ability to cope, and others may stop involving or inviting you, leaving you isolated and with less support.

→ **You miss out on things that matter.** Avoiding activities that you care about due to appearance concerns means missing out on many experiences and opportunities.

→ **It amplifies the Body Bullies.** Avoidance prevents you from realizing that your appearance is just fine and that you can be liked and accepted just as you are. You never find out that the Body Bullies' scary predictions are unlikely to happen, and this reinforces their unkind and inaccurate messages.

Taking care of your body involves finding balance. While spending hours checking your appearance in the mirror is usually unhelpful, avoiding mirrors completely might make you miss important things, like checking if your jacket fits well or spotting something stuck between your teeth. As we continue through this book, we'll explore ways to find the right balance for you.

 Pause and Think **10 Minutes**

Uncover your avoidance and safety-seeking actions

The next step is to think about the people, places and activities that you are avoiding because of concerns about your body or appearance. This can have an impact on friendships and relationships, on study, work, fun and interests.

Avoidance actions	What examples can you think of?	What do you fear will happen?	Safety Actions: What do you do to prevent the fear from coming true?
Avoiding people Do you avoid certain individuals or groups of people? Do you shy away from people you admire, or those you may be interested in dating?			
Avoiding places What places do you avoid? Examples include going to school, the beach, swimming pools, gyms, music festivals or parties.			

cont.

Avoidance actions	What examples can you think of?	What do you fear will happen?	Safety Actions: What do you do to prevent the fear from coming true?
Avoiding activities Do you avoid looking in mirrors, hugging or touching others, eating in public, participating in sports or being the focus of attention, such as when giving presentations or answering questions in class?			
Avoiding reminders of your appearance Do you avoid situations that remind you how you look, such as looking in mirrors, going into changing rooms or clothes stores, or taking photos of yourself?			
What else do you avoid?			

Asha says: I've been avoiding going to Scouts because I'm always worried the wind will blow the hair away from my face and everyone will be able to see how awful I look. I've tried wearing my beanie hat to cover up my forehead, but it makes me hot, and I probably stand out even more when I wear it in summer! I used to have a boyfriend, but I was worried he might try to cuddle or kiss me, which would mess up my hair and make me look awful. My safety actions were to put lots of gel on my hair and to make excuses not to see him, or to avoid getting too close when we were out. In the end, he broke up with me because of this. I was upset because I really liked him.

 **Read This** **10 Minutes**

The impact of unhelpful Appearance Actions

When Appearance Actions become extreme and out of balance, they can have many negative effects on your life. Here's why:

Appearance Actions are distracting. Spending too much time focusing on Appearance Actions makes it hard to concentrate or focus on your usual activities. This can affect your performance at school, work or in hobbies and makes it harder to relax and enjoy yourself in many situations.

They are time consuming and expensive. Appearance Actions can take up a lot of time that may be better spent on many other important or fun tasks and activities. They can also be expensive, especially if you are always seeking the latest cosmetic product or fashion item.

Life can become flat and dull. By doing fewer activities that you care about, life loses a lot of interest and sparkle. It becomes predictable and boring, without much meaning or purpose. This lowers your mood and motivation.

You feel worse about yourself. Believing that your appearance is the most important thing means that you may forget or overlook your talents, interests and good qualities. It's important to remember everything that makes you special, like your skills, hobbies and the people and things you love.

You focus on small details. Constantly checking your body in mirrors, photos or videos encourages you to worry too much about small details of your appearance that most people don't even notice or care about. Remember, everyone has little flaws and they're not as big a deal as you might think.

 **Pause and Think** **10 Minutes**

How do Appearance Actions affect you?

Look back over this chapter and decide which Appearance Actions have the biggest impact on your life. Write a list of two or three actions here:

....

....

....

Now answer the following questions, using a separate column for each Appearance Action you wrote down.

What is the Appearance Action?			
How extreme is this action? How much time do you spend doing it?			
How much effort or attention does it take?			
How easy is it to stop doing this action?			
What important activities does this action make you want to avoid, or make it harder for you to do (e.g. having fun with friends, going to school or doing sports)?			

The first step in building body confidence is to start noticing any unhelpful Appearance Actions that are affecting your enjoyment of life. We will explore some steps for how to make changes in these actions in Part 2 of this book.

Summary: body image and your actions

→ Appearance Actions are the way you react or behave when you have appearance concerns.

→ The three types of Appearance Actions are checking and seeking reassurance, hiding and altering appearance, avoiding and seeking safety.

→ They can be extreme, require effort and take up time, money and attention.

→ Appearance Actions may seem helpful at first, but, ultimately, they create more distress, reduce your body confidence and make it hard to enjoy other things in life.

Final thoughts

Make a note of anything you have found helpful, interesting or surprising from this chapter.

....

....

....

....

....

....

What are you going to do now? Can you choose one small action based on what you have discovered?

....

....

....

....

....

....

Chapter 5

BRINGING IT ALL TOGETHER

So far, we've discovered why you might start worrying about how you look and what can make these concerns stronger. We have also seen how appearance concerns can change the way you feel, think and act. Now, we're going to look at all of this to understand how you see your own body.

So, in this chapter, we will:

→ use a simple 'Body Image Map' to understand how you think and feel about your appearance

→ discover why placing too much importance on your looks has a big role in body image concerns

→ find out why it's good to care less about how you look and more about appreciating and celebrating all parts of yourself.

 Read This 🕐 10 Minutes

Using a Body Image Map

Just like a map shows where you are and where to go, a Body Image Map shows your thoughts and emotions about your appearance and helps you find ways to feel better about how you look. This is the first step towards changing your appearance concerns.

Using a Body Image Map involves looking at five different parts of your reaction.

Parts of your reaction	What to ask yourself	What might you notice?
The situation or trigger	What is happening that is causing you concern about your appearance?	It might be a situation or memory from the past, or something coming up in the future that you are worried about.
What you think	What thoughts and images can you notice? What are the Body Bullies saying?	You might be giving yourself a hard time for how you look, or worrying what others may think of you.
Your feelings and emotions	Which emotions and feelings can you notice?	You might notice many different feelings such as fear, embarrassment, unease, irritation, anger or sadness.
In your body	What sensations can you notice in your body? How much do you focus on your body?	There may be many different body reactions including your heart thumping, tightness in your chest, an ache in your stomach, feeling shaky or sweating, or fast breathing.
Your actions	What actions do you take to prevent or cope with any difficult feelings or to make yourself feel safer? Are there any unhelpful Appearance Actions?	You may be carrying out Appearance Actions such as avoiding certain situations or looking for ways to stay safer, comparing yourself to others, checking your body or seeking reassurance, or trying to hide or alter your appearance in some way.

 **Read This**    **10 Minutes**

Sydney's Body Image Map

Look at the example below, from Sydney, who we introduced in the Introduction to the book:

The situation or trigger: I'm the tallest in my family. I've just had a growth spurt and now I'm the tallest in my year group as well!

What you think
I look like a lanky giraffe.
I look stupid because I'm so much taller than everyone else.
My family are all petite and attractive – why can't I be more like them?
I don't fit in – I don't want to go to parties and stand out.
I'm dull and boring!

In your body
My muscles feel tense, there's a churning in my tummy and I feel sick.
My shoulders and back feel heavy.

Your feelings and emotions
Embarrassed, anxious, self-conscious, uncomfortable, fed up and sad.

Your actions
I try to avoid looking at myself in the mirror.
I have stopped going to parties and social events.
I avoid sports where I might stand out and be noticed.
I don't take photos of myself or post anything on social media.
I hang my head and slump my shoulders so I look smaller.

Sydney says: Breaking it down helped me understand what was going on with me. At first, it was hard to know what to put in each box, but in the end, it started to make sense. I realized that the Body Bullies often show up and have a big effect on my feelings and actions. Attention Grabber makes me focus only on being tall, while Gloomy Gaze makes me forget about everything else except my appearance. I also noticed some unhelpful Appearance Actions: I've been avoiding activities I used to enjoy, like playing sports, which is making me miserable and bored. I'm also trying to hide how tall I am by rounding my shoulders, but that's not working! It's just giving me a backache and stopping me from socializing with my friends!

 Do This  10 Minutes

Create your own Body Image Map

Now choose an example of a recent situation when you felt concerned about your appearance to practise creating a Body Image Map. You can look back at any notes you have made from the exercises in other chapters to help complete it. There is a blank Body Image Map that you can complete using your own examples.

Situation or trigger	What is happening that is causing you concern about your appearance?	
What you think	What thoughts and images can you notice? What are the Body Bullies saying?	
Your feelings and emotions	Which emotions and feelings can you notice?	
In your body	What sensations can you notice in your body? How much do you focus on your body?	
Your actions	What actions do you take to prevent or cope with any difficult feelings or to make yourself feel safer? Are there any unhelpful Appearance Actions?	

What was the situation or trigger?

....

....

....

....

What you think

In your body

What
you think

Situation
and
triggers

In your
body

What
you feel

**Your feelings and
emotions**

Your
actions

Your actions

 Pause and Think   **5 Minutes**

What can you notice?

What do you notice when you break down your reaction using a Body Image Map? Does anything surprise you?	

Are there any links between different areas of the map? For example, do negative thoughts, unpleasant feelings or body sensations lead to you taking unhelpful Appearance Actions?	
Does looking at the map suggest anything that might help you to cope better with your body image concerns? What is this?	

 **Read This**  **10 Minutes**

How important is appearance?

Focusing too much on your outward appearance is often at the heart of body image problems. We live in an image-conscious world, where social media, advertising and peer pressure push you to prioritize looks over other important aspects of life. Body Bullies like Attention Grabber and Cruel Critic amplify this by insisting that 'appearance is everything' and that you must always look 'perfect'.

When appearance becomes too important, it can seriously affect your emotions and life. You may feel insecure, low in confidence and unhappy in your own skin. You may ignore or overlook all the great things that make you individual and unique and find it hard to appreciate your body for its strengths and all the incredible things it allows you to do.

You get trapped into spending a lot of time and energy thinking about your body image, constantly focusing on what you don't like, comparing yourself to others and looking out for criticism or negative reactions.

Remember, this does not mean that you should stop valuing your body or taking care of your appearance. It's normal to feel frustrated when your hair won't behave, to use concealer on a spot or to wonder whether your thighs look wobbly in leggings. Nevertheless, your appearance mustn't become the most important thing in your life. You don't need to give it 100 per cent of your time, effort and attention.

Think back to some of the people we have talked about so far and the impact of their appearance concerns.

Vihaan: I focus on my appearance and what I am wearing a lot of the time instead of thinking about my fitness and friendships.

Charlotte: I spend ages trying to fix my face in the mirror instead of concentrating on my schoolwork. I was predicted to get good grades but now I'm not sure I will even pass!

Asha: I love nature and the outdoors, but I worry about my hair blowing about in the wind, looking awful and showing my large forehead, so I never go hiking with friends any more.

What important things are you missing out on by putting too much attention on your appearance? Are you getting into a battle with your body? Does it help to compare yourself with the images you see in the media?

 Pause and Think  **10 Minutes**

Has your appearance become too important?

Use the following table to think about how important your appearance has become to you:

What else is important in your life? Make a list of some other things in life that you care about, such as people, places or activities that matter to you.	
Now think of these *other* things as slices of cake, with each piece representing how much effort and attention you give to different parts of your life. How big would each slice be?	
How big would the slice of cake be that represents how much attention you give your appearance?	

> Your appearance chart – draw out how much time and energy you give to different parts of your life, including your appearance.

Vihaan's appearance chart

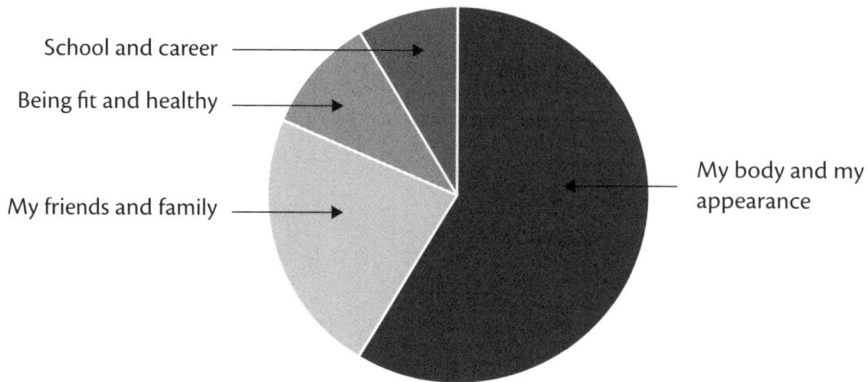

School and career

Being fit and healthy

My friends and family

My body and my appearance

What did you notice from your appearance chart? Is your appearance slice too big?	
How could you get more balance in your chart? What do you need to concentrate on more? What do you need to do less of?	
Can you plan to do one small action that might create a little more balance in your life?	

 **Read This** **5 Minutes**

Learn to accept your body

Developing body confidence isn't about perfecting your looks. It's about accepting and appreciating your body as it is, rather than constantly trying to change it, and recognizing that your value goes well beyond your appearance, no matter what the Body Bullies say!

Body acceptance doesn't mean giving up caring about your appearance. But acknowledging and appreciating your uniqueness can boost your wellbeing, self-esteem and confidence. This leads to a healthier and more balanced approach to self-care, valuing your body for its strengths and the amazing things it allows you to do.

It can be tough not to get caught up in negative thoughts and the Body Bullies' loud demands and criticisms. But you don't have to believe or act on their negative messages. You don't even have to argue with them or convince them that you look OK. Maybe you do have a big spot on your nose today! Maybe your nose isn't perfectly straight, or your hair doesn't look exactly like the pics on social media. These things can be true, and you can still be an amazing, unique and worthwhile person who takes pride in their individuality.

Acceptance means not buying into the idea that you must look a certain way to be OK. You can start to recognize that your personal value isn't tied to your physical appearance and that you are more than enough, just the way you are.

> **Ross:** Over-valuing my appearance was getting me nowhere, cutting me off from my friends and making me miserable. I decided to try to accept that I am smaller than others, and just be who I am. I started agreeing with anyone who said I was small and thin by saying 'yeah ... and that makes me fast too... and I'll give you a sprint race any time...' That worked well and made me feel less anxious and threatened because I stopped dreading the focus being on me. When I accepted my body and appreciated it a bit more, the conversation changed and moved on.

Building body confidence takes time. In the next section, we will discover some practical GROWTH skills to tackle the Body Bullies and start to build your body confidence.

Summary: bringing it all together

→ Focusing too much on your appearance is often at the heart of body image problems.

→ A Body Image Map can help to make sense of your appearance worries and reactions by looking at five areas:

> the situation or trigger

> what you are thinking

> your feelings and emotions

> what's happening in your body

> your actions.

→ Accepting and appreciating your body is the first step to increasing body confidence.

Final thoughts

Make a note of anything you have found helpful, interesting or surprising from this chapter.

....

....

....

....

....

....

What are you going to do now? Can you choose one small action based on what you have discovered?

....

....

....

....

....

....

Part 2

10-MINUTE GROWTH STEPS TO BEFRIEND YOUR BODY

Chapter 6

WHAT ARE THE GROWTH STEPS?

Next, we will meet the six 10-minute GROWTH steps that can help you boost your body image and feel more confident in your own skin. We will look at each one in more detail in the following chapters. These steps don't have to be followed in order. You might also need to go back and forth between chapters several times, as you face new situations and challenges.

Here's an overview of the steps:

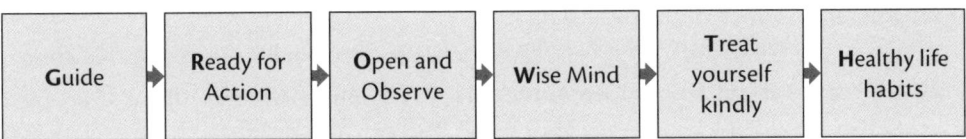

 ## Follow your Guide

The first step is to meet your Guide. This is like an inner compass that helps you focus on the important things that you care about most rather than giving too much time and attention to your body or appearance. Following your Guide involves asking yourself: 'Who and what do I care about? What kind of person do I want to be? What do I want out of life?'

You will meet your Guide in Chapter 7, where you will start to explore some of the things that motivate, interest and inspire you.

Ready for Action

Being Ready for Action involves changing what you do and how you act. Doing activities that are important or enjoyable can lift your mood, increase your energy and happiness, and distract you from uncomfortable thoughts or feelings about your appearance.

Getting Ready for Action involves planning and doing things that follow where your Guide is pointing. You can experiment by trying things out, testing how it feels to do them, discovering what happens and whether they fit with who you want to be. You don't have to be certain what the outcome will be, and it may take time and many tiny steps to achieve an important life goal.

You will start getting Ready for Action by setting yourself some small goals to do things that matter to you in Chapter 8.

 ## Open and Observe

Learning to Open and Observe involves noticing what's going on inside you and in the world around you. Being able to recognize your thoughts, feelings and actions can help you to understand yourself, make sense of how you are reacting in any situation, and decide whether this is helpful or unhelpful. You will learn how to tune in to what you feel in your body and notice your thoughts, feelings and urges to react in certain ways. This might involve deliberately paying attention to something or shifting your focus from your appearance onto something else.

You can use Open and Observe skills to help you step back from constantly churning over worries about your appearance and learn to ignore the negative voices of the Body Bullies when they show up in your mind. This can also help you to appreciate and enjoy what is happening in the here-and-now rather than worrying about things in the future or going over events from the past.

You will start practising Open and Observe skills in Chapter 9.

 ## Wise Mind

Your mind is your inner voice and includes your thoughts, beliefs, ideas, expectations, memories and personal stories. It is an incredibly powerful and useful tool that can allow you to make complicated decisions and plans. However, at other times, your mind may become critical and negative. You may find that the Body Bullies bring harsh or judgemental thoughts about how you look, which drain your confidence and make you feel fed up, anxious and ashamed.

Using Wise Mind involves starting to notice whether your thoughts are balanced, fair and helpful and choosing which ones to pay attention to. You can learn to step back from extreme or negative thoughts and find ways to tune out unhelpful or self-critical thinking patterns that may be keeping you stuck, draining your body confidence and making it harder to do things that matter to you. You can choose to notice more helpful thoughts, such as remembering your strengths and good qualities, and allow these to influence your actions and choices, rather than focusing only on your body and appearance.

You will discover more about your Wise Mind in Chapter 10.

Treat yourself kindly

Are you friendly and encouraging to yourself or do you give yourself a hard time and become stuck in body shaming and self-criticism? Learning to treat yourself kindly involves being supportive, kind and fair to yourself, and balancing three different emotion systems, which all have an important part to play in your health and happiness:

→ **Threat system:** This will alert you to possible danger and help you quickly take action to stay 'safe' or comfortable, but if you overuse this system, you can feel tense, stressed and agitated.

→ **Drive system:** This energizes and motivates you, helping you seek out opportunities and achieve your goals. If you don't use this system effectively you can feel demotivated and find it hard to get important things done. You might also spend too much time focusing on one area of your life and ignore other important achievements.

→ **Calm and Connect system:** This helps you feel peaceful, contented, calm and safe. It helps you to feel close to other people and to recover when facing problems or when things go wrong. If you don't use this system enough, you can become self-critical and give yourself a hard time when thinking about your body and appearance.

You will discover how to balance these systems and banish your self-critic in Chapter 11.

Healthy life habits

Building healthy life habits involves making choices about your daily routines that look after your health and your body. This can make you feel happier, more energetic, less anxious and better able to achieve the things that are important to you. Healthy life habits include eating patterns, being active, getting enough sleep, looking after your body and your technology habits.

We will explore healthy life habits in Chapter 12.

 Pause and Think **5 Minutes**

What's next?

What do you take away from this introduction to the six GROWTH steps? Do any steps feel more important for you? You can choose which chapters you focus on next, but we recommend that you start with Chapter 7, which will introduce your Guide. This is a helpful starting point that can build your motivation and help you focus on what you care about.

Summary: overview of the GROWTH steps

This chapter introduced the six 10-minute GROWTH steps:

→ **G**uide: Focus on who you want to be and what you care about most.

→ **R**eady for Action: Prepare for change and take small steps towards what matters.

→ **O**pen and **O**bserve: Be more aware of what's going on in your mind, body and the world around you.

→ **W**ise Mind: Get perspective and choose helpful ways to react to different situations.

→ **T**reat yourself kindly: Balance your emotion systems and banish your inner critic.

→ **H**ealthy life habits: Create healthy routines that encourage your wellbeing.

Final thoughts

Make a note of anything you have found helpful, interesting or surprising from this chapter.

....

....

....

....

....

....

What are you going to do now? Can you choose one small action based on what you have discovered?

....

....

....

....

....

....

Chapter 7

FOLLOW YOUR GUIDE

Grace: I used to be full of fun, always smiling and laughing, but these days I just feel lost and unsure. When I look in the mirror, I can hardly recognize myself. My nose seems too big, my lips are too thin and my body isn't shaped right. The more I look at myself, the more my appearance looks wrong. It makes me feel so sad and empty. I get frustrated, I keep having arguments with my parents and I'm not interested in anything that I used to enjoy. It's like I don't know who I am or what to do with my time except for staring in the mirror and trying to fix all the problems that I see there.

 ## Meet your Guide!

Your Guide is like an inner compass that points in the direction of people and things that are important to you. When you are struggling with appearance concerns, you may lose confidence and cut down or avoid many activities that make life fun or bring a sense of purpose. You might forget or ignore many of your personal qualities because the Body Bullies insist that the only thing that matters is how you look. You might be stuck carrying out endless Appearance Actions like mirror checking, comparing yourself to others or trying to hide or alter how you look. These can stop you from doing things that matter to you and leave you feeling lost and confused.

This is where your Guide can help. Finding your Guide involves thinking about your *values* – the people and activities that you care about most. It also involves discovering what is important to you and what gives your life *meaning* and *purpose*. Following your Guide involves choosing actions that take you in the direction you wish your life to go, even if this involves effort and overcoming challenges.

In this chapter, we will meet your personal Guide and discover answers to the following questions:

→ What is most important to you in life? What direction is your Guide pointing in?

→ How can your Guide help to boost your body confidence, reclaim your life and feel more fulfilled and contented?

→ How can you start doing more things that matter even when you may feel anxious or embarrassed about your appearance?

 Pause and Think **5 Minutes**

What is important to you?

Getting to know your Guide involves asking yourself some 'big' questions. Look at some of these below.

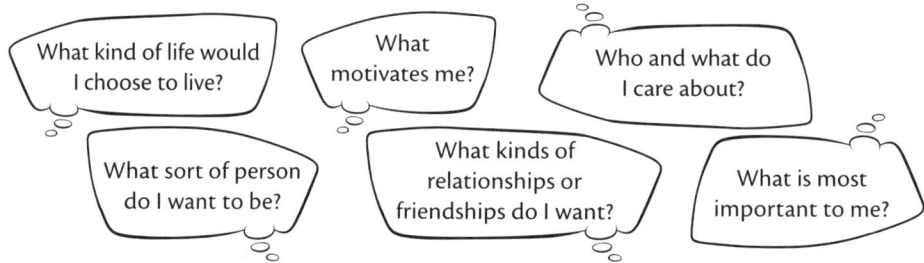

What immediately comes to mind? Don't worry about getting the 'right' answer, as there will be lots of chances to change and develop your ideas throughout the book.

Write your first thoughts here:

....

....

....

....

....

....

....

....

 Read This  10 Minutes

Why do values matter?

Life can be full of pressures, like schoolwork, hobbies and social life, often while you're going through personal changes or dealing with life stresses and problems. This is all made even more difficult when you're constantly worried about how you look.

Thinking about what you value most can help guide your choices, especially during tough times. In fact, this is exactly when it can be most important to follow your Guide. When you are feeling fearful, stuck, confused or overwhelmed, your Guide can motivate and inspire you to make helpful choices, remember what's important and keep going when facing life's difficulties.

Knowing your values can help you to make choices that match with who you want to be as a person. If you value friendship, kindness or social connection, it's worth making the effort to meet up with a friend who is struggling, even when your hair is not quite right, or if you haven't had time to perfect your make-up. If you value physical exercise or the outdoors, it's worth the effort to get outside and go for a bike ride or a hike even if you are tired after a busy week, or when you are worried that you might look hot and sweaty afterwards.

What are your values?

Take a few minutes to look at this list of values. Rate how important each one is to you from 1–5 (where 1 is not very important and 5 is extremely important). Aim for around four to six very important values (scoring 4 or 5) right now. You can change your choices at any time and add any important values that are missing.

Values	How important? (1–5)	Values	How important? (1–5)
ACCEPTANCE: being accepted for who you are and accepting others		**INDEPENDENCE:** being able to make your own decisions and choices	
ACHIEVEMENT: making progress towards important accomplishments and goals		**INDIVIDUALITY:** to express yourself as a unique person, celebrating diversity and difference	
ACKNOWLEDGEMENT: to matter, to be appreciated, seen and heard by others		**KINDNESS:** being friendly, caring and encouraging to yourself and others	

cont.

Values	How important? (1–5)	Values	How important? (1–5)
ACTIVE: participating in physical activities, exercise, dance, movement or sports		**RELATIONSHIPS:** having close personal, romantic and/or sexual relationships	
ADVENTURE: having new and exciting experiences		**LEADERSHIP:** taking responsibility for making decisions and guiding others	
BELONGING: feeling part of a friendship group, community, team, organization, culture, family		**LEARN and GROW:** making progress, developing skills and discovering new knowledge	
BODY and HEALTH: taking care of your body, health and appearance		**NATURE:** the outdoors, animals and the natural world	
CALM: finding peace and tranquillity in your life		**ORDER:** being organized, following or developing a pattern or routine	
CARE: looking after yourself and others		**SAFETY:** finding physical and emotional safety, security and predictability	
CHALLENGE: solving problems, stretching your limits and testing your abilities		**SPACE:** finding freedom, reducing restrictions and demands in your life	
CONNECTION: affection, warmth and closeness with important people in your life		**SPIRITUALITY and RELIGION:** following important beliefs and traditions	
CONTRIBUTION: giving your time and using your skills in ways that feel important or meaningful		**TEAMWORK:** working in a group with shared goals	
CREATIVITY: expressing or enjoying creativity in different ways, including music, writing and art		**TRUST:** honesty, fairness and being able to trust those around you	
FINANCE: having security and money to spend as you choose		**VARIETY:** seeking out new and different experiences	
FUN: humour, laughter and enjoyment		**WORLD MATTERS:** politics, global or environmental issues	

Other important values? list these here:		Other important values? list these here:	

 Pause and Think **5 Minutes**

Did you find it easy or difficult to choose your values? Was it hard to stick to only four to six important values, or did a few seem a good 'fit'?

....

....

How does it feel to think about your values? Have you discovered anything important or useful?

....

....

Grace: Figuring out my values was tricky because I've never really thought about them before. At first, all I could think about was my appearance since I spend so much time worrying about how I look. However, eventually, I realized other things matter to me too. I care about my family and being close and connected with them. I know my mum worries a lot about me, which makes me feel bad. I used to be really creative and energetic – I've always loved music and dancing, but I stopped going to classes because of the skimpy leotards that made me self-conscious. Having fun is important to me too. I used to love hanging out with my friends, laughing and being silly together. Now, I hardly ever see them.

 **Read This** **5 Minutes**

Key facts about values

Here's a quick reminder of some important facts about values and your Guide.

Values are...	Values are not...
✓ directions not destinations; they are about the route that you follow on your journey, not where you end up.	✗ goals to achieve or things to tick off your to-do list.
✓ flexible ideas that change over time as you grow and develop and can be adapted to suit circumstances.	✗ fixed rules about what you 'should' do, or what's 'wrong', 'right', 'good' or 'bad'.
✓ your qualities that reflect the type of person you want to be and what you appreciate in yourself and others.	✗ always easy and can involve making difficult choices or experiencing uncomfortable feelings.
✓ personal and may be similar, overlapping or completely different to the people around you.	✗ meant to always fit in with other people's values or mean you ignore your own beliefs and opinions.

 **Read This**    **5 Minutes**

Talk about your Guide

Just talking about your Guide can help you find a sense of purpose and improve your mood and confidence. Who could you chat with about what matters to you? It could be someone in your family, a friend or someone you trust such as a teacher or youth leader. Show them this exercise and your list of values and use this to get the conversation started. How are their values similar or different to yours?

Make a note of what you discover here:

. . . .

. . . .

. . . .

. . . .

. . . .

 **Read This**    **10 Minutes**

Living your values

Now that you've met your Guide, you can start planning 'Towards Actions' which move you in the direction of important values. A value is a general direction rather than a specific goal or target. You can't tick values such as 'independence', 'relationships' or 'fun' off your to-do list, but you can plan and carry out actions that are linked to each of these areas. If you value learning and growth, then goals might be to read a book, pass an exam or learn how to fix a car engine. For creativity, your goal might be to paint a picture, make some music or write a story. Living out your values can boost your energy, lift your spirits and help you feel more contented and fulfilled.

Taking a Towards Action often involves getting through some discomfort. Planning a walk with a friend could move you towards important values such as connection and being active, but it may also involve overcoming difficult feelings like anxiety, tiredness, sadness or boredom. You might also have to pull yourself away from Appearance Actions such as checking in the mirror or scrolling through social media.

'Away Actions' are the opposite – they move you away from the things you care about. Examples include not completing an important piece of coursework because you're stuck doing an endless skincare routine, or missing out on seeing your best friend because you are embarrassed by a big spot on your nose.

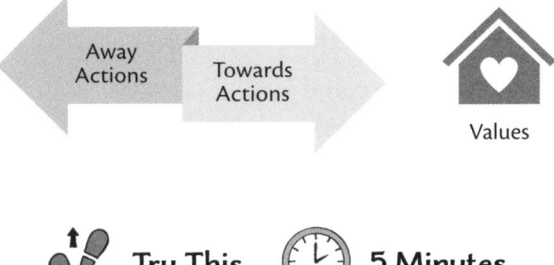

🐾 **Try This** 🕐 **5 Minutes**

Take a towards step

In Chapter 8, we will look in more detail at setting goals and planning actions. For now, can you think of just one small action that would take you towards an important value? Make sure it is quick and easy to complete and takes no longer than a few minutes.

Write it here:

....

....

....

....

....

....

Grace: I decided to try to take one small step towards one of my values. I know my mum worries about me, so I suggested that we go to a local café at the weekend. It's only a small café so I don't feel too worried about going there, and we used to go all the time. My mum is very supportive, and it would be good to spend some time with her. I'm also planning to listen to music a bit more. I put on one of my favourite songs today – I haven't listened to it for ages! It always makes me feel more upbeat and like myself again.

If you are wondering if taking one small action will make any difference, don't worry! The aim is not to fix all your problems at once. This is just the first small step towards something that you care about!

 **Read This** **10 Minutes**

 ## Follow your Guide through hard times

It's even more important to keep following your Guide when you are struggling with body confidence or feeling low, anxious or embarrassed about your appearance. You can focus on your values and keep doing things that matter to you, even if difficult thoughts or feelings pop up on the way. This is like surfing a wave and staying on your board, feeling the thrill of riding over it, or riding your bike over a bump in the road and continuing to stay on track, knowing that this will improve your confidence and how you feel.

 Pause and Think **5 Minutes**

Following your Guide through discomfort

Think of a time when you felt apprehensive or nervous about doing something but did it anyway because it was important. You could choose a time that you spoke up for someone, completed a sports challenge, took an exam or went into a new situation.

Describe the situation. What happened? What did you do?	

What uncomfortable thoughts and feelings did you overcome to do this?	
What were your important values? Were you following your Guide?	
What was the long-term effect of overcoming these difficult thoughts and feelings?	

 **Try This** **10 Minutes**

Are your values clashing?

Sometimes it can seem that your different values are clashing or competing. If you value learning, you might set yourself a goal to pass an important exam. Each evening you'll need to decide how to use your time. Should you study? Get some exercise? Eat a healthy meal? Go out with your friends? Or take time to relax and sleep?

Making these decisions will depend on lots of things: How soon is the exam? Are you hungry or tired? Will exercise help you concentrate? How much have you studied already this week? You'll also need to consider other values like activity, connection and fun.

Sometimes, one value becomes too dominant. Are you focusing too much on appearance and neglecting other areas? Is this affecting your relationships or activities?

The aim is to find a balance between different values. This might take time to achieve, but if a value is important, it's best not to ignore it completely. There's no perfect answer – experiment and be ready to adjust your plans. Sometimes you can satisfy several values at once like going for a walk in the park (outdoors/active) and chatting to a friend on the phone at the same time (connection) or while listening to a podcast (learning/enjoyment).

Keep updating your values and the direction your Guide points as you grow and develop through life. Revisit this chapter regularly and notice how your values evolve.

Pause and Think  **10 Minutes**

Balancing your values

Look again at the four to six most important values that you chose previously. Write them down here:

....

....

....

....

....

....

Now answer these questions.

Have you forgotten, overlooked or ignored any important values recently? How might you start to bring them back into your life?	
Are any values becoming overwhelming, demanding or holding you back in some way? How can you balance these with other values?	

Grace: I asked my mum to go to the café with me and she was happy to go. On the day, it was hard to pull myself away from the mirror and I felt very anxious about whether my make-up was OK. I have some blemishes on my face, and I wasn't sure if they were completely covered up. I did my make-up for about half an hour, but then I stopped and we went out. Usually, I take an hour or even longer to get ready, or I might not go at all! It felt quite stressful at first, but we got to the café, and I focused on eating my favourite cake, which was delicious. In the end, I was glad I went, and it was nice to spend some time with my mum.

94

 Read This  10 Minutes

Look for meaning and purpose

Many people seek happiness, yet striving too hard to find it can leave you feeling stressed and frustrated, or feeling that you are falling short. It's often more rewarding to look for purpose and meaning. This involves looking outwards, finding ways to make a difference in the world and getting involved with things that are bigger than you are. By contributing to the wider community, you may feel more fulfilled, contented and optimistic, and cope better when things go wrong.

It can help to connect with like-minded individuals – to find a tribe of people who understand your point of view. Finding even one person who shares your values can make a difference. You might discover a whole community – whether face-to-face, online or through shared beliefs like a campaign or faith group. Together, you can encourage and support each other.

 Try This 10 Minutes

Finding your sense of purpose

Look at this list of ways to increase your sense of meaning and purpose in life. Which could you try?

Ideas for finding meaning and purpose	Examples	What could you try?
Connect with others, finding ways to share your hopes, fears, successes and failures.	Talk to an understanding friend or a supportive adult about the things that are most important to you, or listen to someone else who is struggling.	
Give some time to your local community.	Find a way to volunteer your time and get involved. Could you support your local parkrun, volunteer with an animal shelter or join a local community youth group, Scouts or Guides?	
Step up to a new challenge and develop new skills and experiences.	Sign up for a leadership position at school or college or learn a new skill that can benefit others, such as first aid.	

cont.

Ideas for finding meaning and purpose	Examples	What could you try?
Get involved in a cause that you care about.	Find ways to make your family or school greener, join a lifesaving club or a local environmental group, or call out discrimination when you see it.	
Find ways to explore the world around you.	Join a new club or activity, apply for a part-time job, learn a new language or explore your local area with friends.	

Summary: using your Guide

→ Your Guide points towards the things in life that matter most to you.

→ Living your values involves taking Towards Actions that move you towards an important value, even if these involve overcoming challenges or feel difficult at first.

→ Your goal is to find a balance between different values and to stop body image concerns from getting in the way of what's important.

Final thoughts

Make a note of anything you have found helpful, interesting or surprising from this chapter.

....

....

....

....

What are you going to do now? Can you choose one small action based on what you have discovered?

....

....

....

....

Chapter 8

GET READY FOR ACTION!

Rhys: I've always had problems with eczema, but lately it's been affecting my life a lot. I'm constantly checking my skin in the mirror and my brain zooms in on every small patch of dry skin. I worry that there are huge, ugly, red patches and that they look flaky and awful. When I go out, I imagine everyone is staring and feeling disgusted. I wear long sleeves to cover my arms and I comb my hair forwards to hide my face. Sometimes I pick at my skin, which can leave even more red marks. I used to be very active and played a lot of tennis. I even volunteered as a tennis coach at our local club, which was great for getting involved with matches and social events. However, lately, I've struggled to find the motivation to play at all. It's hard to even leave my room sometimes, and I avoid social events because I'm scared people will judge me for my awful skin. It feels like I'm trapped, missing out on everything I used to enjoy, and I can't seem to find a way out.

 Getting Ready and Taking Action involves doing more things that matter to you. When you are struggling with body image concerns, you can get stuck in a pattern of unhelpful Appearance Actions such as checking your appearance, asking for reassurance, comparing yourself to others or avoiding scary or uncomfortable situations. As we have already learned, this often ends up making you feel worse over time. You can miss out on fun and exciting things and start to feel unhappy and trapped by the Body Bullies.

The good news is that you can break free of this habit by paying less attention to negative thoughts and adding a few fun or interesting activities to your day. Making small changes can help you feel better about yourself, improve your mood, boost your energy and help you enjoy life more.

So, in this chapter we will learn how to:

→ do activities that are important, enjoyable or meaningful, even if you are also dealing with uncomfortable thoughts and feelings about your appearance

→ choose actions that can boost your confidence, lift your mood and increase your energy and enthusiasm

→ plan small changes or 'micro-steps' that are easy to achieve

→ swap unhelpful Appearance Actions for more positive and fun activities.

 Pause and Think 10 Minutes

Which activities are important to you?

You can use your Guide like a compass to help you decide which activities are most important. Ask yourself these questions.

Where is your Guide pointing? What matters to you? Write down two to three important values. Turn back to Chapter 7 for a reminder if you need to.	
Write down some examples of activities that are linked to each of these values.	
Imagine you could wave a magic wand and feel energetic, enthusiastic and confident. How would you spend the day? What would you do?	
What activities did you enjoy or do regularly in the past? What have you stopped doing?	

Here are Rhys's answers.

Where is your Guide pointing? What matters to you? Write down two to three important values. Turn back to Chapter 7 for a reminder if you need to.	I care about being fit and active, especially playing tennis. I also like using my tennis skills to coach younger kids. It makes me feel proud of my achievements and I liked being part of a team at the club. Spending time with people who share my interests makes me feel connected.
Write down some examples of activities that are linked to each of these values.	Playing and coaching tennis! Hanging out with friends from the club. Doing other activities and sports.

Imagine you could wave a magic wand and feel energetic, enthusiastic and confident. How would you spend the day? What would you do?	I would grab my racket and ask one of my friends to hit a ball around the local court! Maybe I'd try a new sport where I could learn some different skills and get to know new people. I've always wanted to try judo. I don't want to stay stuck at home staring in the mirror!
What activities did you enjoy or do regularly in the past? What have you stopped doing?	I used to enjoy computer coding. I would spend ages working on different codes – it's like I get to create my own world, or it's like solving a complex puzzle. But because I've been feeling fed up, I haven't got round to doing it lately.

 **Read This**    **10 Minutes**

Change your actions with 'micro-steps'

An easy way to take control of your life is to use 'micro-steps'. These are tiny, easily achievable changes to your actions. Each micro-step takes only a few minutes to complete and does not involve anything difficult or overwhelming.

Breaking down bigger tasks or challenges into small, easily achievable steps can build your confidence and self-belief. These small steps can be repeated regularly to create positive habits and will help you to make progress towards bigger goals.

You can carry out a micro-step even if you have feelings of anxiety, self-doubt or embarrassment about your appearance. Maybe the Body Bullies show up in your mind, giving you a hard time and trying to control your choices. They may tell you to stop trying anything new and fall back into the safe routine of repeated Appearance Actions. *But* ... even if the Body Bullies show up, you can still choose to carry out important actions. By behaving 'as if' you feel a little less anxious, you may find that you start to feel more confident too.

When planning a micro-step, remember to be specific about what you are planning to do. Ask yourself the following questions:

→ **What** are you planning to try?

→ **When** and **where** will you try it?

→ **Who** or **what** can help you achieve this step?

→ **What skills** can you use to help you cope with any difficulties or challenges?

→ **How confident** are you that you can achieve this? How can you make your goal smaller or easier? Who can you ask for support to complete it?

 Try This  5 Minutes

Plan your micro-steps

Look at the box below with some examples of micro-steps. Pick two or three ideas. Can you commit to carrying these out within the next few days? Remember, each one should take only a few minutes to complete.

Examples of micro-steps	What are your ideas? Can you carry this out in the next few days? When will you do it?
Message a friend to see how they are. Make a healthy snack or a drink. Cuddle a pet. Doodle or draw for a few minutes. Listen to a song you like. Go for a 5-minute walk round the block. Look up a new recipe to try. Practise five basketball shots in the garden. Play a quick video game. Dance to some upbeat music.	

Rhys: I can see that many of the actions I was thinking about trying were pretty big – not really micro-steps – so I wasn't feeling confident I could carry them out! I'd love to play tennis, but it feels hard to jump straight to playing a match. A micro-step could be to get my racket out and hit the ball against the wall in the garden for a few minutes. That feels a lot less daunting. It would be good to build up my fitness, so I could try a few minutes of jogging, or even just take the dog for a walk in the park. My dad was talking about doing the couch to 5k, so maybe we could try that together. I could also send a message to my friend. It would be good to be less isolated and cut-off from everyone.

 Pause and Think 10 Minutes

Notice what happened

After you try a new activity, it's useful to think about what you achieved and give yourself a pat on the back. If for some reason it didn't happen, it's also helpful to think about why, and if there is anything useful to learn from this.

If you achieved, or mostly achieved your goal, ask yourself the following questions.

What did you plan to do? What did you end up doing?	
Was this action following your Guide? What important values was it linked to?	
What was the effect of doing it? How did you feel afterwards?	
What might be the effect in the future from doing it?	
How can you build on any success? What will you try next?	

If things didn't go according to plan, you can also ask yourself these questions.

What got in the way? For example: I ran out of time, I forgot, it was too hard or something else came up.	
Is this still something important to you? If not, what else could you try?	
Do you need to make the action smaller or easier? Can you get some help or support to do it? How can you remember to do it?	

 Pause and Think  **10 Minutes**

Use SPICE to balance your activities

Sometimes it can be helpful to expand the range of things you do and include activities that are good for your health and wellbeing. This isn't about trying to change how you look but about focusing on using your body to enjoy yourself and have fun. You can do this by adding some **SPICE** to your day or week! These involve one of the following types of activity:

→ **S**uccess or achievement

→ **P**hysical activity and moving your body

→ **I**mportant or meaningful for you

→ **C**onnection or closeness to others

→ **E**njoyable, relaxing and fun.

The following table includes examples of different types of SPICE activities. Put a tick against the ones you might try. You don't have to do everything in one go or finish the whole activity – you can take a micro-step – but do try to cover all the types of activity over a week or so. Add any of your own ideas and interests to the list.

Type of activity	Examples	What are your ideas? What could you do?
Success or achievement	Try a new recipe or an old favourite. Learn something new. Sign up for an acting class. Build a website or write a blog. Finish a project you've been putting off. Rearrange your bedroom. Write a poem, rap or a short story. Tick something off your to-do list.	
Physical activity and moving your body	Go jogging, running or for a bike ride. Go for a swim or to the gym. Jump on a skateboard or roller skates. Bounce on the trampoline. Dance to a song. Practise football, tennis or basketball. Do an online workout. Mow the lawn or do some gardening.	
Important or meaningful for you	Volunteer for a local charity. Take your driving test or learn first aid. Watch an online lesson. Learn to repair your bike. Apply for work experience or a job. Campaign for a change in the world. Go to the dentist.	
Connection or closeness to others	Invite friends for a movie night. Cuddle or play with your pet. Message or FaceTime someone. Play a board game. Make a card for a friend or grandparent. Go window shopping with someone. Look at photos of your favourite people.	

Enjoyable, relaxing and fun	Play an instrument or listen to music. Watch a comedy or a funny video. Do a puzzle or craft activity, or construct something. Massage some cream into your hands or feet. Take a long shower or a bubble bath. Stroke a pet or a soft cushion.	

Rhys: Looking at the list of SPICE activities made me realize that I've stopped doing a lot of things that used to be fun. In fact, I'm not doing much at all! I'm spending so much time trying to cover up my eczema or check how bad it is, that I hardly do anything else. I'm going to try a few different micro-steps. I'll start by trying to get back into coding – I'm planning to spend just a few minutes coding something very simple. I might also invite my friend to watch a movie. I'd really like to learn to drive next year so I could ask my parents about making a start with my driving theory test.

 **Read This**  **5 Minutes**

Create a routine

One way to get more active is to make it part of your daily routine. You can start by keeping a record of your activity levels using your phone, a diary or a planner. This will help you to keep track of your achievements and can motivate you to continue making new changes.

Take some time each week to look through your diary and check how you are getting on. This will help to keep yourself on the right track. As your new patterns of activity turn into habits, it will become easier to do them. Make sure your routine is flexible and can adapt to any new situations or events. We talk more about ways to create healthy life habits in Chapter 10.

 **Try This** **10 Minutes Per Day**

Using an activity diary

Can you practise keeping track of your daily activities over the next few weeks, using the diary template below? Notice whether they are SPICE activities. What effect did the activity have on your mood – how did you feel after doing it?

Day		What was the activity? How long did you do it?	Was it a SPICE activity? Success or achievement Physical activity and moving your body Important or meaningful for you Connection or closeness to others Enjoyable, relaxing and fun	How did you feel after? Rate your mood from 1–10
Monday	Morning			
	Afternoon			
	Evening			
Tuesday	Morning			
	Afternoon			
	Evening			
Wednesday	Morning			
	Afternoon			
	Evening			
Thursday	Morning			
	Afternoon			
	Evening			
Friday	Morning			
	Afternoon			
	Evening			
Saturday	Morning			
	Afternoon			
	Evening			
Sunday	Morning			
	Afternoon			
	Evening			

Pause and Think  **10 Minutes**

At the end of each week, ask yourself the following questions.

What can you notice about how you spent your time this week?	
Are there any links between any activities and how you feel each day? Did any activities make you feel more positive or lift your confidence, mood or energy?	
Can you start to plan short SPICE activities to fill any gaps in the week ahead?	

Rhys: I was surprised that it was so helpful to keep a diary of my activities. In the beginning, I didn't have much to write in it! Then I started noticing small micro-steps that I was doing, and I got motivated to add in a few more. I found that some activities like coding are easy to focus on, so time flies by and I hardly think about my skin at all. Other activities like exercise are also a great distraction from the Body Bullies and they also make me feel more energetic and positive afterwards. I like being able to look back and see everything I've done over the week – it gives me a big boost and a feeling of accomplishment.

 **Read This** **10 Minutes**

Swap or reduce your Appearance Actions

Alongside increasing SPICE activities, the next step is to start reducing how much time you spend on unhelpful Appearance Actions like checking in the mirror, asking for reassurance, or avoidance. Spending too long on these actions will often have a negative effect on your mood and can distract you from other important things.

At first, you could aim to reduce the time you spend on each type of activity by 5–10 minutes. You can then build this up over the next few weeks or months. The ultimate aim may not be to stop completely but to cut it down to a level where it's not dominating or interfering with other parts of your life. This is about getting balance and making sure you are following your Guide towards all the parts of your life that are important.

 Pause and Think **10 Minutes**

Swap Appearance Actions for SPICE activities

Look at the following list. Which Appearance Actions can you recognize? How much time do you spend on them? Can you swap these for more positive or enjoyable SPICE activities? You may need to experiment with different types of activity and see which ones are most helpful. Make sure that you are planning small and achievable micro-steps!

Type of Appearance Action	How many minutes do you usually spend on this each day?	What change can you plan to make? E.g. reducing by 5–10 minutes	What SPICE activities could you try instead?
Checking your appearance, for example in mirrors or by touching or measuring your body			
Comparing yourself to photos or videos or people around you			
Talking to people about your appearance or asking for reassurance about how you look			
Putting on or adjusting make-up, skin products or styling your hair			

Using or researching cosmetic treatments or supplements to try to change your body or appearance			
Avoiding people, places, activities or reminders about your appearance, or using safety actions to prevent your fears from coming true			

Rhys: I was shocked when I worked out that I spend 2–3 hours each day on Appearance Actions. Nevertheless, although I knew I should cut down, it wasn't easy. The Body Bullies can be very loud, and the urge to check myself in the mirror is so strong that it feels almost impossible to ignore. I started by trying to cut down my mirror time by just 5 minutes, which felt easier than stopping completely. I found that being active was the best way to take my mind off my skin, and I always feel happier and more energetic afterwards. Watching TV didn't work so well, because I still thought about my appearance a lot. Playing a computer game was better – it was easier to concentrate on this and I didn't get pulled back to the mirror so quickly. It's only been a small change so far, but I feel pleased I have a plan and that I'm starting to make progress!

Summary: Get Ready for Action!

→ Getting Ready for Action involves doing things that are important, enjoyable or meaningful.

→ 'Micro-steps' can help to build your confidence as you achieve many small successes.

→ Swap out your unhelpful Appearance Actions for more positive and enjoyable SPICE activities that follow your Guide.

Final thoughts

Make a note of anything you have found helpful, interesting or surprising from this chapter.

....

....

....

....

....

....

What are you going to do now? Can you choose one small action based on what you have discovered?

....

....

....

....

....

....

Chapter 9

OPEN AND OBSERVE

Mei Lin: I can't seem to stop thinking about how I look. Every morning, I spend ages getting ready for school, trying to get my make-up right and hide any spots or blemishes. I also hate my nose – I think it's too big and I can never get my hair just right to hide it. I used to laugh these thoughts off or ignore them, but lately it's been harder to think about anything else. Even when I'm in a lesson that I like, or talking to a friend, my mind keeps drifting back to my appearance. I keep wondering if anyone is staring or laughing at me. It's hard to concentrate on what the teacher is saying or join in when my friends are chatting and laughing. It feels like I'm stuck in a loop of constant stress and worry about my appearance, and it's really getting me down.

Learning to Open and Observe involves paying attention to what's going on inside you and in the world around you.

With appearance concerns, it's easy to spend a lot of time and energy thinking about how you look. Do you find it hard to stop obsessing over possible flaws or problems with your body? Do you spend a lot of time comparing yourself to others, or are you constantly on the lookout for possible criticism or negative reactions from those around you? Does this make it harder to focus on other things or stop you from enjoying important activities?

Next, we will practise being present in the here-and-now. Instead of being dominated by the Body Bullies, or lost in distressing thoughts and feelings, you can start to notice these without being overwhelmed. Stepping back and observing can help you break free from unhelpful Appearance Actions and enjoy life more fully.

In this chapter, we will:

➜ discover the impact of fixating on your appearance

➜ learn some skills to ignore the Body Bullies and keep your attention on track by noticing what else is happening in your body and mind, and the world around you

➜ find ways to get more involved and enjoy your daily activities.

Do you fixate on your appearance?

If you spend a lot of time fixating on your appearance, it becomes extremely hard to pull your attention away from thoughts about how you look.

You might begin by noticing some thoughts or worries, such as:

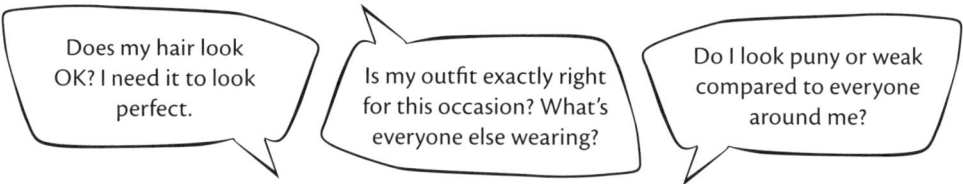

Does my hair look OK? I need it to look perfect.

Is my outfit exactly right for this occasion? What's everyone else wearing?

Do I look puny or weak compared to everyone around me?

Attention Grabber and the other Body Bullies will often then show up and make things even worse, saying things like:

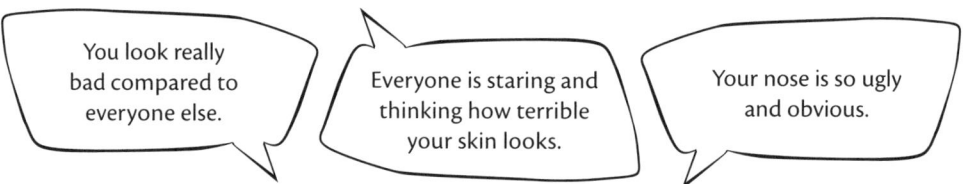

You look really bad compared to everyone else.

Everyone is staring and thinking how terrible your skin looks.

Your nose is so ugly and obvious.

We discovered in Chapter 3 that negative thoughts can be like watching a movie inside your mind. Fixating on your appearance is like being trapped watching a film that makes you feel bad about yourself. The Body Bullies have turned the volume up to the max, and the movie seems very vivid and realistic. It's hard to see or hear anything else. It's impossible to remember all the things that you like about yourself that you can be proud of.

Watching this upsetting movie on repeat can make you feel insecure and unhappy in your own skin. You might want to leave, but it's hard to find the exit in this dark and gloomy movie theatre. So, you stay glued to your seat, watching the movie over and over again. You are stuck fixating on your appearance.

Pause and Think  **10 Minutes**

Do you ever find yourself getting trapped in the movie theatre and fixating on your body or appearance? Can you think of a time that this happened recently?	
What was happening in the movie? What thoughts or images were showing? Which Body Bullies were watching with you?	
How did it feel to be watching this movie on repeat?	
How did it affect you to get stuck in appearance fixation? Did it make it harder to concentrate on the activity or task at hand?	

Mei Lin: I can really relate to the movie theatre idea. It feels like I'm chained to my seat, unable to get away from all the negative thoughts and worries about my nose. It makes me upset and frustrated, and it's starting to get in the way of doing other things. I find it hard to enjoy myself with friends, and my schoolwork is even starting to be affected. I don't want to be stuck watching this boring and negative film! I want to find my way to the exit or change the movie so I can get on with my life!

 **Read This** **10 Minutes**

Hard to focus on what's important

Getting caught up with worries about how you look can distract you from other parts of life. In class, you might not hear the teacher because you are thinking about the photo you posted on social media last night. In sports, you might get distracted by thinking about whether your legs look strong enough, or if your thighs look wobbly when wearing shorts, so you miss a shot or don't play at your best.

Being fixated on your appearance makes it harder to join in conversations. It's difficult to think of something interesting to say if you are busy worrying about your hair or make-up, comparing yourself to those around you, or worrying about a spot on your chin. This can knock your confidence and you may start to believe that you are not very socially skilled – when it's simply that you are just not paying attention.

Getting fixated on one feature or aspect of appearance can also mean that you exaggerate small flaws and see them as worse than they really are like Mei Lin worrying about her nose. Often this will be very different to how others see you.

Worries about how you look can also make it hard to pay attention in school or at work, which can affect your grades. It can also make it tough to focus on hobbies, sports or other activities. Even when you're trying to relax or wind down, these thoughts can pop up and make you feel stressed and irritable.

 Pause and Think **10 Minutes**

When do you fixate on your appearance?

Look at this list of situations. How often do you get stuck fixating on your appearance rather than paying attention to the activity at hand? Does this affect how much you can concentrate or enjoy the activity or task?

When are you likely to fixate on your appearance?	Can you think of a recent example? Describe it here:	What was the impact of getting fixated? Could you concentrate on or enjoy the activity?
Social situations such as chatting with friends or family, individually or in groups		
When you are trying to listen or concentrate on studies or a complicated task		
When you are doing sports, activities or something fun		

When others are paying attention to you, such as when you answer a question in class, give a presentation, perform or compete		
When you are trying to relax, wind down or fall asleep		
Any other situations?		

 Read This 10 Minutes

How can Open and Observe help?

Open and Observe is about learning to be mindful. This means learning to pay attention to your thoughts, feelings and what's happening around you. This can help you worry less about your looks and focus on other things.

Using Open and Observe is not emptying your mind or trying to get rid of all your worries. You can't just erase difficult thoughts and feelings or stop the Body Bullies from appearing in your mind. However, you can notice them, let them be and give them space to pass in their own time. This way, they won't bother you as much, and you'll be able to enjoy positive and enjoyable things in life more.

 Try This  30 Seconds

Take a slow sip of water

Pour yourself a glass of water. Find a comfortable seat somewhere quiet and peaceful. Pick up the glass and hold it for a few seconds, noticing its smooth surface. Does it feel warm or cool in your hands? Notice the shape of the glass and any colours that you can see. Now take a small sip. Hold the water in your mouth for a few seconds before you swallow. Pay attention to its temperature, texture and taste. Then swallow and let the water flow smoothly down your throat.

What sensations did you notice? What did you see, hear, touch, taste or smell?	
Did any thoughts show up in your mind? Did you notice any feelings or emotions?	

Congratulations! You were *Open* to sensations, thoughts and feelings and able to *Observe* them for a few seconds!

 Read This  5 Minutes

Work out your attention muscle

Using Open and Observe involves noticing when you have become stuck in the appearance movie theatre, fixating on your looks and then trying to pay more attention to what you're doing. Like exercising a muscle, the more you practise attention and focus, the easier it will become. This doesn't have to take a lot of time. Just a few minutes, or even a few seconds, each day can help you become more aware and better able to handle difficult thoughts and feelings.

Here are some short activities that will help to build Open and Observe skills:

 Try This 2-10 Minutes

Pay attention to daily activities

Practise doing an everyday activity, such as taking a shower or brushing your teeth, with a little more focus and awareness. This might help turn a routine or boring activity into something that gives you a little more satisfaction or creates a sense of calm. It helps if you use all your senses: vision, sound, taste, smell and touch. Experiment with some of the following suggestions.

When to use Open and Observe skills	What could you do?	Can you try this? Where and when will you do it?
During a shower or bath	Notice the warmth and refreshing flow of water and breathe in the smell of your favourite shampoo or shower gel.	

Brushing your teeth	Listen to the sounds and notice the sensations and minty taste as you brush around each tooth and your gums.	
Being active, walking or moving your body	Can you notice your feet on the ground, your legs moving, and the sensation in different muscles as you stretch your arms above your head or gently touch your toes?	
Talking to someone	Focus on the person you are talking to. Notice the sound of their voice and the words they are saying. Can you say something that shows you have been listening?	
Listening to music or sounds around you	Can you notice two or three sounds around you? What are the loudest and quietest sounds you can hear? If you are listening to music, can you notice the lyrics, then switch to different instruments, the beat or rhythm?	
Eating and drinking	Can you notice the smell, temperature and texture? Pause before swallowing and feel the sensations as the food or drink moves down your throat.	
Any other regular daily activity	What else can you choose to pay attention to?	

 Pause and Think **10 Minutes**

Pick one or more examples to try. Can you commit to doing this for a few seconds to a few minutes at least two to three times a week for 2 weeks?	

How could you remember to do this? Can you set an alarm on your phone or leave a Post-it note as a reminder?	
After you've practised for a while, what can you notice? Is anything different?	

 Try This **3–10 Minutes**

Mindful breathing

Sit comfortably with your eyes closed or look down at the ground in front of you. Breathe in and then allow a long sigh as you breathe out slowly. Let your body settle and start to feel heavier.

Notice your breathing. You might be able to feel air moving through your nostrils, across your upper lip or at the back of your throat. Maybe you can feel the rise and fall of your chest or the gentle movement of your belly up and down with each breath.

Gently focus on one area of your body where you can notice your breathing. Notice each breath in and each breath out, and the short pause in between.

Can you bring a kind attitude to this practice? You could wish yourself well in dealing with all the challenges that life brings.

When you find your mind wandering, just gently bring it back to the next breath with friendliness and patience.

Mei Lin: I decided to try using Open and Observe while brushing my teeth in the morning because that's a tough time for me – I often get really focused on my appearance, and it makes it hard to leave the house. I had to set an alarm on my phone to remind me! Normally when I brush my teeth, I stare at my face and nose in the mirror. This time, I focused on other sensations. I noticed the minty smell and taste of the toothpaste and the sound of the cool water running from the tap. I felt the gentle pressure of the toothbrush moving in my mouth. My mind did drift back to the mirror a few times, but I turned away which helped me stay focused on brushing. Afterwards, it was a bit easier to move on to the next part of my morning routine. I'm going to keep it up and try using Open and Observe during breakfast too.

 **Read This** 5 Minutes

Flexing your attention

Open and Observe skills can also help when you've become stuck doing unhelpful Appearance Actions, such as spending too much time on social media or looking in the mirror. Instead, you can practise 'flexing your attention'. This involves keeping your mind open and flexible, rather than becoming fixated by thoughts or an activity.

You can work on this by paying attention to what's happening around you and then switching your focus to your own thoughts or feelings. Then shift your attention back out to your surroundings as you look around and decide what to do next.

 **Try This** 1–3 Minutes

Practise flexing your attention

Practise this attention-flexing exercise for a few minutes each day:

→ Notice or create a sensation in your body. Push your feet into the floor, scrunch your toes or stretch your arms above your head. Pause for 5–10 seconds and notice how it feels.

→ Now move your attention to a sound for 5–10 seconds. It might be something you can hear around you, or you can create a sound by gently humming or tapping on the desk.

→ Shift your attention to something that you can see. Take 5–10 seconds to look at this, noticing the colours, shapes, shadows and textures.

→ Now flex again and notice what's happening inside you. Can you name an emotion? What's going through your mind? Is there anything that you have an urge to act on, like hunger, thirst, an itch or stiffness?

→ Finally, can you widen your attention to notice several things at the same time? This might include physical sensations, sounds, thoughts, emotions or what you can see.

Now ask yourself: What have you discovered? What's the most important thing to focus on next in your day?

 Read This　⏰ 5 Minutes

Noticing and appreciating

You can also use Open and Observe skills to get better at noticing even tiny moments of happiness or contentment in your day. Your brain is programmed to look out for risky, stressful or negative events to try to avoid danger and keep you safe. This is a survival instinct, but it also means that you may overlook more enjoyable parts of life.

Instead, you can take a few minutes to think about anything that you appreciate and enjoy. It's like shining a torch on something colourful, beautiful or interesting on a dark damp night. You could even show your body some appreciation for the hard work it has completed during the day!

 Try This　⏰ 2-5 Minutes

Appreciate something small

Take a few minutes to notice and appreciate the small things in your day:

➜ *I see...* Focus on something you enjoy looking at – a beautiful view, a loved one's face, a garden full of flowers, an interesting building or images related to your interests like science or games. Notice the colours, shapes and patterns. Take a slow breath and appreciate using your vision to experience the world.

➜ *I smell... I taste...* Think of a taste or smell that you love. Imagine enjoying the flavour and texture of that food or drink, and breathe in the smell deeply. Consider the people involved in bringing it to you – from growing and harvesting to transporting and selling. Send them a moment of thanks and appreciation.

➜ *I am touching and feeling...* Focus on something you like to hold or feel. It could be warm water in the shower, a pet you love to stroke, or some soft, calming material. Try stroking your arm from the shoulder to the hand, or placing a hand over your heart, noticing the warmth and the pressure, and wishing yourself well.

➜ *Thank your body...* Take a moment to appreciate your body for all its effort and hard work each day. Think about how every part of your body helped you achieve what you did today.

 **Try This** **2-5 Minutes Per Day**

Keep a gratitude journal

Keeping track of small things that you appreciate or are grateful for can boost your happiness and wellbeing by highlighting enjoyable parts of life that you may otherwise overlook. Here's how to get started:

→ Choose a notebook or journal or use your phone or laptop to record your thoughts.

→ Set a specific time each day to write, whether it's in the morning, after school or college, or before bed. The important thing is to do it regularly.

→ Note two or three things you appreciated, enjoyed or felt grateful for that day.

→ Be specific about what happened and why you appreciated it. You don't need to write a lot, just enough to remember the event later.

→ Allow yourself to absorb any positive feelings like contentment, happiness or peacefulness as if you're taking a warm bath or shower.

→ Keep it simple. Focus on small moments and experiences, not just major events. It could be as simple as enjoying a meal, a kind word from a friend, noticing a beautiful view or hearing a favourite song. If you can't find three things, one will do! Just making the effort to focus on something you appreciate will make a difference.

Mei Lin: I spend a lot of time worrying, so it was quite a change to try a gratitude journal. I bought a pretty notebook to encourage me to use it more often. I often get anxious in the evening, so I decided to try writing in my journal at bedtime. Here's what I wrote:

1. My friend sent me a funny meme today, which made me laugh during a tough study session.

2. My maths teacher was kind when I didn't understand one of the problems. She spent time explaining it after class and didn't make me feel stupid for not getting it right away.

3. I noticed some daffodils growing by our house. They looked so pretty and made me feel that spring is on the way. I appreciate how my eyes allowed me to see them!

I was surprised at how nice it was to write these things down. It was a nice way to relax before bed. Reading them back afterwards made me feel warm and happy. I'm going to make it a regular habit.

Summary: Open and Observe

→ Open and Observe involves noticing your reactions and the world around you.

→ You can practise by paying attention to everyday activities for a few minutes each day.

→ Try flexing your attention if you get stuck in one activity or point of view.

→ You can also notice moments of contentment and happiness in your day.

Final thoughts

Make a note of anything you have found helpful, interesting or surprising from this chapter.

....

....

....

....

....

What are you going to do now? Can you choose one small action based on what you have discovered?

....

....

....

....

....

Chapter 10

WISE MIND

Lucas: I've always been aware of my crooked teeth, but it never used to stop me from asking questions in class, especially if I liked the subject. Now that I'm in a big, mixed college, I feel a lot more self-conscious. I worry that I look like a geek or an idiot, and I imagine everyone is staring at my teeth and laughing. When this happens, I feel embarrassed and start blushing or trip over my words, so I've been holding back during class discussions. I'm studying languages and want to be a journalist, so I really need to be able to speak out and share my opinions. Lately, I've been doubting if I have what it takes to finish the course.

 Your mind is your inner world and is made up of many thoughts, beliefs, stories and images which help you to make sense of the world. It develops and changes throughout your life and is shaped by many things including your personality, family background, people around you and events in your life.

Other people cannot see your mind, but it will influence how you feel and act. When you have appearance concerns, your mind often becomes harsh and critical, and you may spend a lot of time thinking negatively about your body.

Developing Wise Mind is very different to listening and reacting to the negative stories of the Body Bullies. It involves looking at the big picture, being friendly and fair to yourself, and thinking flexibly, looking for ways to appreciate your body and make the most of your life.

In this chapter, we will:

➔ learn to tune out the Body Bullies and take less notice of their unhelpful opinions

➔ discover that you have a choice about which thoughts to listen to and what actions to take

➔ strengthen your Wise Mind and discover more balanced and fair ways of seeing yourself and the world.

Spot when the Body Bullies are bossing

The first step in using Wise Mind is to *notice* what's going on in your mind. What thoughts have shown up? Can you spot the Body Bullies? Are they bringing thoughts into your mind that are exaggerated, mean or hurtful? Have you got stuck watching distressing movies about your appearance on repeat?

In Chapter 3, we talked about calling out the Body Bullies by NAME so you can notice when they are around and choose to react differently to them. Your Open and Observe skills can help by allowing you to notice where your mind is and keep your attention flexible.

Here are some more ways to turn down the volume of the Body Bullies:

Try This 2 Minutes

Label your thoughts

Say your thoughts aloud or write them in a journal, on a Post-it note or your phone or computer. Observing your thoughts will not make them disappear but it can make them less powerful and overwhelming. You can experiment with changing the size, font and colour, and see if this alters how much you believe the thought.

You could use one of these phrases:

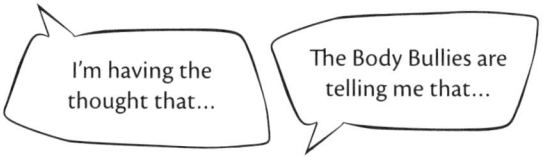

I'm having the thought that…

The Body Bullies are telling me that…

Remember, you don't have to believe everything that the Body Bullies are telling you! If you pause and wait, you may find that more positive or fair thoughts also start to appear.

No matter what thoughts show up, you can choose how to react to them. Ask yourself: 'What's the most helpful action I could do next?'

 **Try This**  **5 Minutes**

Say 'So what?' to the Body Bullies!

This technique helps sharpen your awareness and create a pause, which allows you to quickly recognize when negative thoughts and the Body Bullies are trying to boss you. Instead of reacting impulsively, take a step back and observe. Here are the steps:

Stop and spot the Body Bully: Pause and breathe out saying the word 'so' in your mind. Notice what's happening in your mind. What are the Body Bullies saying? What is the most difficult thought, image or memory?

Observe and tune out the Body Bullies: Take a few slow breaths without reacting immediately. Use your other senses to step back from negative thoughts. What can you see, hear or touch around you? Now, imagine scrolling past the Body Bullies like an annoying status update on social media. You don't have to argue with them or react to what they say. Picture the Body Bullies playing on a movie screen that shrinks down to the size of your phone. The movie is still there, but it's smaller and quieter. Put it in your pocket and continue with your day.

What is important? Finish by choosing an action that follows your Guide towards something you care about. Remember, you have the power to choose how you respond to negative thoughts!

 **Read This**  **5 Minutes**

 ## Meet your Wise Mind

Your Wise Mind is like a best friend or a supportive coach or teacher who motivates you through encouragement, kindness and wisdom, unlike the Body Bullies who shame and criticize you. Your Wise Mind sees and appreciates your whole self – recognizing your attributes, qualities and skills.

Wise Mind believes that you can succeed if you keep trying and encourages you to look for solutions to problems and to keep going even if things don't work out at first. Along with your Guide, Wise Mind will also motivate you to do important things, even if you are feeling anxious, scared or embarrassed.

When facing difficult situations, your Wise Mind:

→ **is more than skin deep:** Wise Mind values your abilities and good qualities, not just your looks

→ **sees the bigger picture:** it helps you focus on what's most important to you

→ **has a supportive attitude:** even when something has gone wrong, when you are not looking your best, or when you are facing something stressful, scary or difficult

→ **empowers you:** it helps you feel strong and capable in challenging situations.

 Pause and Think   **10 Minutes**

Who inspires your Wise Mind?

Wise Mind will develop throughout your life, as you experience different life events and challenges. Everyone benefits from support and encouragement in dealing with problems, and your Wise Mind is somewhere you can always turn to.

To develop your Wise Mind, it can help to think about anyone that you admire or find inspiring.

Think about people you trust for good advice or support. It could be an inspiring teacher, coach, friend or family member.	
Consider who else inspires you. It could be a sportsperson, someone who has overcome challenges, a talented singer, a historical figure	
Think about one individual that you have listed above. What do you find helpful or inspiring about them? Focus on their good qualities, rather than their appearance. Is it their courage, strength, focus, determination, kindness, fairness or something else?	
What wise words would any of your inspiring figures say to you or to others who were struggling? How would they advise or encourage you? How could this help you cope with your appearance concerns?	

 **Pause and Think**  **10 Minutes**

A peaceful and wise space

You can also turn to nature to inspire Wise Mind. Try this activity to find an image that helps you to feel strong and focus less on your appearance as you navigate through stressful emotions and difficult life experiences:

➜ Imagine you are in your favourite space. This might be a beautiful garden, high in the mountains, sitting on a warm beach looking out to sea, in a forest or staring up at the stars at night.

➜ Look around and notice what colours and shapes you can see around you. What sounds can you hear? What can you touch and feel? How does it feel to be in this place that you love?

➜ Can you imagine that this place is happy that you are here? This is a place that wants to support and encourage you, and accepts you just as you are, without wanting or expecting you to look a certain way.

➜ How does being in this supportive space affect how you see the world and see yourself? What images or ideas can encourage your Wise Mind to speak up a little more and support you through tough times?

Lucas: I've always looked up to my dad when I've been struggling with problems, but sometimes he doesn't really get how I feel. I'm starting to want to be more of my own person, making my own decisions and not relying on my parents' point of view. So, I decided to choose something else for my Wise Mind. I love the outdoors and when I feel insecure or self-conscious, I picture a strong, powerful mountain. I also think of my ski instructor, who helped me navigate down a mountain during a scary snowstorm. He was calm and encouraging, guiding the way and making it clear he believed in me. I always remember his words: 'You've got this … you're doing great!'

 Read This   10 Minutes

Compare is unfair!

It's natural to notice how others may look similar or different to you, but spending too much time comparing yourself to others can negatively affect your emotions and your body image. Comparisons cause problems because of the following:

→ **They use unfair standards:** You are often comparing yourself to digitally enhanced or unrealistic images on social media or the internet, which don't reflect real people in the real world. This can lead to dissatisfaction with your appearance, low self-esteem and anxiety.

→ **They highlight the negatives:** When you compare yourself to others, you tend to focus on what you lack or dislike about your appearance, rather than appreciating how well your body works and your positive qualities. This crushes your self-confidence.

→ **It's impossible to relax:** Constant comparisons make you stressed because there's always someone who seems thinner, taller, slimmer, more muscular or who has better hair. This makes it hard to feel comfortable in your own skin.

→ **Everyone is unique:** Your appearance is a unique blend of genetics, lifestyle and personal choices. It's impossible to look exactly like anyone else, or like the idealized images you may see. Appearance is *not* everything! Try to appreciate and celebrate your unique features and what *your* body can do.

Imagine the positive impact if you eased up on comparing yourself to others and instead focused on accepting yourself and doing things that you enjoy.

Next, we will explore some ways to help you develop your Wise Mind, recognize your self-worth and embrace the life you have in your unique body.

 Read This   5 Minutes

Strengthen your Wise Mind

Has someone ever told you that you're smart? Funny? Kind? Artistic? A caring friend? A good student? A talented writer? A promising athlete? Do you acknowledge these compliments and feel proud, or do you just brush them off and focus on your appearance instead?

To develop your Wise Mind, you can start to notice and appreciate your skills, accomplishments and unique qualities. Your Wise Mind sees you as a whole person who is not just defined by your appearance. Your looks are just one small part of who you are.

Focusing on your strengths might feel uncomfortable at first, but with practice, recognizing your good qualities can boost your personal pride and inner confidence.

 Pause and Think **10 Minutes**

Notice your skills and qualities

Complete the table below with some of your strengths and qualities. This exercise is not about being vain, it's about seeing the real you and acknowledging the parts you can be proud of. Think broadly and include strengths and qualities that go beyond looks. If you find it difficult, you can ask a supportive friend or relative for help.

What are some of your strengths?	
What are you good at?	
What do you enjoy and care about?	
How can you appreciate and use these qualities in your life even more?	

 Pause and Think **10 Minutes**

Your strengths checklist

Your strengths are not just related to your achievements but include many other qualities such as being honest, trustworthy, fair and caring for others. Look at the list below and choose at least four or five strengths and qualities that you recognize. Choose a recent example of each and think about how you can appreciate or develop this quality.

Strengths and qualities	What is a recent example?	How can you grow this quality or use it in your life?
I was caring or friendly.		

cont.

Strengths and qualities	What is a recent example?	How can you grow this quality or use it in your life?
I was fair or honest.		
I acted as a leader.		
I was curious or interested in something.		
I understood someone else's point of view.		
I learned something new.		
I worked hard or overcame an obstacle or problem.		
I gave good advice or support to someone.		
I coped with some difficult emotions or thoughts.		
I was energetic or active.		
I was careful or I planned ahead.		
I was brave in the face of stress or danger.		
I spoke up for what was right.		
I was creative.		
I forgave someone else, or myself.		
I understood a fact or some information.		
I had fun or brought a smile to someone's face.		
I completed something.		

 Read This  10 Minutes

Your body is amazing!

One way to overcome appearance concerns is to focus less on how your body looks and more on what it allows you to do. Your body is incredible! Can you appreciate that it enables you to live and enjoy activities that bring you happiness?

Think about your body's amazing abilities. If you love art or music, value how your hands create beautiful drawings or play a musical instrument. If you enjoy sports, appreciate how your body lets you run, climb, swim or perform gymnastics.

Your body does many things without a conscious effort, such as breathing, hearing, laughing, talking, seeing, touching, hugging a friend or stroking a pet. Can you start to see your body as a powerful tool rather than just an object to be looked at?

 Pause and Think  10 Minutes

Appreciate what your body can do

Answer these questions to help you recognize and appreciate your body's amazing abilities.

Ways to appreciate your body	What can you think of? How can you use this?
Enjoyable activities: Write down some things that your body can do that you enjoy, such as dancing, playing an instrument, running, hiking or any other physical activity.	
Notice sensations: How does it feel to do activities you enjoy, such as playing a sport, being creative or making something with your hands? Notice the sense of accomplishment and any positive emotions.	
What surprises you? Can you recall any times when your body surprised you with its strength, resilience, capability or agility? What were you able to achieve? How did this make you feel?	

 Read This   🕐 10 Minutes

Zooming in on 'flaws'

Focusing on one small part of your body that you don't like – like the shape of your nose, a blemish on your skin, your height or body hair – can negatively impact how you feel about yourself. Here's why zooming in on flaws causes problems:

→ **It makes you feel bad:** Constantly worrying about one specific flaw will make you anxious and stressed and affect your self-confidence and mood.

→ **It warps your view:** Focusing intensely on one area can distort your perception, like shining a powerful spotlight on one small area, which makes things seem much worse than they really are. You might also start to believe that this one small issue defines your entire appearance, which isn't true.

→ **You ignore the good stuff:** By fixating on one flaw, you overlook all the positive things about your body and how healthy you are.

 Pause and Think    **10 Minutes**

Zoom out and see the big picture

Think of a time when you zoomed in on a small part of your appearance that you didn't like or were worried that others might use to judge you. Start by noticing how it feels when you focus on this from close up.

What thoughts do you have? What are the Body Bullies saying? For example: My nose looks crooked and ugly.	
How does it make you feel when you think about this? For example: I feel embarrassed and anxious.	
Can you notice any sensations in your body? For example: My belly starts churning and my chest feels tight.	

What urges to take action can you notice? What does this make you want to do? For example: I want to look at my nose in the mirror and check if I can fix my hair to try and hide it better.	

By zooming out, you can see the bigger picture and appreciate your whole self.

Take a few slow breaths and close your eyes. Imagine you are standing in a vast open space, like a big field or a beach that stretches out to the sea. Now rise into the air – maybe you jump into a helicopter or fly up like a superhero.

As you look down, see yourself sitting far below. Notice how tiny your body looks from high up, and how the problem that you were concerned about shrinks too. The higher you go, the smaller and less important it becomes. Eventually, it disappears altogether.

Now look around and take in the vast landscapes and the expansive sky. Marvel at the world that is so much bigger than your worries. See the earth stretching out in all directions, full of diverse landscapes and endless opportunities.

As you slowly come back down, remember that your flaw is just a tiny unimportant part of who you are. Focus on what your body can do and the amazing things it allows you to experience. You are so much more than your appearance. You are a unique individual with immense potential, part of a big world with many exciting adventures ahead.

What did you notice as you rose upwards? Did you see yourself any differently from high above?	
What does your Wise Mind say? What is a more balanced and realistic way of seeing yourself?	
How might this change your actions? What can you do differently because of your new knowledge and perspective?	

Lucas: I tried this exercise, and it helped me see things differently. From high above it was easier to stop obsessing about my teeth. Wise Mind reminded me that no one has ever said anything bad about them, and my dentist says I take good care of them. From high above, I could see all the other things that I'm interested in. I don't want my worries to stop me from doing well in my spoken Spanish exam. I want to travel the world and meet new people. My teeth help me eat, enjoy food and to speak. I have lots to say and I want to express myself without constantly worrying about my appearance!

 Pause and Think **10 Minutes**

Make wise choices

Although you can't control which thoughts pop into your mind, you can always choose how you behave or what actions you take. Wise Mind encourages you to follow your Guide and make wise choices about your actions.

Use the table below to think through a recent example of a time that you felt fearful or down about your appearance.

What happened? What was the situation?	
What thoughts went through your mind? Which Body Bullies were loudest?	
How did you feel? What emotions or body sensations could you notice?	
What did you do? What Appearance Actions did the Body Bullies want you to carry out?	
What might be the effect of acting in this way repeatedly or for a long time? How might this affect your confidence or how you live your life?	

 **Try This**  **10 Minutes**

Choosing wise actions

First pause and take a few slow breaths, using your Open and Observe skills to settle any strong emotions. Now ask yourself these questions.

What's important? Do your actions fit with your values and follow your Guide? What skills and strengths could you call upon?	
What does Wise Mind say? What would you say to a friend or family member who was struggling with the same situation? How might a supportive coach encourage or motivate you, or help you find courage or inspiration?	
Can you find perspective? Can you rise high above the situation? Do things look different from up there? Can you step back and consider what matters?	
What choices do you have? Can you choose a helpful or wise action, even if you still have negative thoughts or feelings? What actions might build your confidence and improve your life rather than seeking short-term relief from discomfort?	

Lucas says:

What happened? What was the situation?	I was chosen to read a poem I wrote at an end-of-term celebration.
What thoughts went through your mind? Which Body Bullies were loudest?	Cruel Critic really ripped into me telling me that my teeth are discoloured and look disgusting when I read aloud.

How did you feel? What emotions or body sensations can you notice?	I felt really tense and my face felt hot. I was upset because it was an honour to be chosen and I'm passionate about poetry and writing.
What did you do? What Appearance Actions did the Body Bullies want you to carry out?	I wanted to avoid the situation, so I didn't embarrass myself. I made an excuse and told the tutor I didn't want to do it.
What might be the effect of acting in this way repeatedly or for a long time? How might this affect your confidence or how you live your life?	If I keep listening to the Body Bullies, I'll never be able to do the things I want to in life! It's going to sap my confidence and I will feel fed up and down because I'm not living the life I really want to.

Lucas: I used Open and Observe skills to pause. I stretched out my arms above my head, listened to sounds for a few seconds and took a sip of water. Then I tried to find my Wise Mind to answer the next few questions.

What's important? Do your actions fit with your values and follow your Guide? What skills and strengths could you call upon?	I'm proud of my poem, and I know how excited my parents would be to hear me reading it aloud. The poem was about the environment – something I feel strongly about – and I'd like to share it with others.
What does Wise Mind say? What would you say to a friend or family member who was struggling with the same situation? How might a supportive coach encourage or motivate you, or help you find courage or inspiration?	Wise Mind encouraged me to make the most of this opportunity. In the future, I want to be a journalist and inspire people with my writing. I would tell a friend that if it's important to them then they should just have a go. What they say matters much more than what they look like!
Can you find perspective? Can you rise high above the situation? Do things look different from up here? Can you step back and see what really matters?	I visualized myself standing steadfast and solid looking down at the world from the top of a mountain. This reminded me of adventurers I admire and helped me feel braver. What really matters is this is a great opportunity for me!
What choices do you have? Can you choose a helpful or wise action, even if you still have negative thoughts or feelings? What actions might build your confidence and improve your life, rather than seeking short-term relief from discomfort?	I still feel nervous but I'm going to talk to the tutor about giving it a go. She is always very encouraging and helps me feel more confident. I'm going to give it a try!

Summary: Wise Mind

→ Listening to Wise Mind involves being friendly and fair to yourself and recognizing your qualities, skills and positive attributes.

→ Saying 'So what?' to the Body Bullies allows you to step back and observe them rather than getting pulled into doing what they say.

→ Zoom out and see things from a distance, appreciating your body for everything it can do, rather than taking a close-up view that focuses too much on appearance.

→ No matter what thoughts and feelings show up, you can choose wise actions that follow your Guide towards the things that matter.

Final thoughts

Make a note of anything you have found helpful, interesting or surprising from this chapter.

....

....

....

....

....

....

What are you going to do now? Can you choose one small action based on what you have discovered?

....

....

....

....

....

....

Chapter 11

TREAT YOURSELF KINDLY

Holly: My body image issues started when I was being bullied. A group of girls constantly picked on me, saying mean things or hiding my bag at lunchtime so I could never find it. At home, I'd stare in the mirror thinking that everything about my appearance was wrong – my messy hair, unstylish clothes and shapeless body. I tried hard to improve my looks, hoping the girls would be nicer, but the bullying continued. I started believing I could never fit in, and I stopped putting effort into my studies. Even after the bullies left the school, I shut myself away in my bedroom, telling myself that I was stupid and ugly and that no one liked me. I felt completely worthless.

When struggling with appearance concerns, you can often see yourself and your body in the worst possible light. You become self-critical, comparing yourself negatively to others, and blaming yourself for everything that you don't like about your appearance.

Body Bullies like Cruel Critic may show up bringing unkind or hurtful thoughts like, 'I'm useless,' 'Nobody likes me,' 'I'm fat,' or 'I'm ugly.' However, saying mean things to yourself can be just as hurtful and damaging as saying them to someone else. Getting into a habit of putting yourself down or calling yourself names can severely impact your body confidence and worsen appearance concerns.

Self-critical thinking often gets worse when you are facing problems like bullying, discrimination or abuse. You can find yourself echoing the negative voices and telling yourself the same harsh messages. You might also struggle with self-criticism if you have unrealistic or unreachable expectations. Are you never satisfied with anything less than perfection, and feel like a failure if something small goes wrong? Do you expect yourself to appear flawless, with no room to relax or take a day off from striving for perfection?

In this chapter, we will:

→ discover your three emotion systems and how they influence your mind and body

→ learn how treating yourself with kindness can help you cope with appearance concerns, making you stronger and better equipped to handle life's challenges

→ practise ways to turn down the volume of the Body Bullies and become a better friend to yourself.

 **Read This**   **5 Minutes**

The three emotion systems

Different emotion systems work together to create a balance in your body and mind that helps you feel confident, happy and content, and cope with stressful life events and challenges. The three systems are:

→ Threat

→ Drive

→ Calm and Connect.

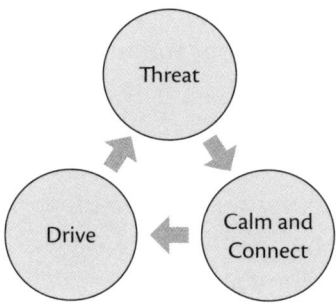

 **Read This**  **10 Minutes**

Threat system

The Threat system is your inbuilt survival system. Its job is to alert you to possible danger and keep you safe from harm. Whenever you face any kind of stressful or threatening situation, your Threat system will wake up, and by releasing hormones such as adrenaline and cortisol, it tells your body to take immediate action and stay safe.

The actions you take when the Threat system is activated are known as Fight Flight Freeze:

→ **Fight:** You get ready to defend yourself and combat the danger.

→ **Flight:** You try to avoid, escape or run away from the danger. You might also try to stay safe by checking for danger or staying close to someone else.

→ **Freeze:** You feel stuck, frozen and unable to move, as you stay completely still to avoid detection.

You can experience many different emotions when the Threat system is activated, including fear, anger, disgust, embarrassment and shame. Your body will start preparing to take Fight Flight Freeze actions, so you may notice that your heart starts thumping in your chest, you breathe faster, you start sweating, shaking, feeling sick or get a stomach ache.

Is your Threat system too touchy?

The Threat system is designed to respond quickly to danger, whether you are facing a bully, taking a difficult exam or jumping out of the way of a speeding car. When you have appearance concerns, your Threat system can become overly sensitive to how you look. It's like having a super-powered radar constantly scanning for flaws. When it detects something, even if it's something very minor, the alarm sounds loudly, often blowing things out of proportion.

The Threat system doesn't just react to what you see in the mirror. The alarm can be triggered every time you have harsh or self-critical thoughts about your appearance. Body Bullies like Cruel Critic can attack you from within, saying how unattractive you are or how bad you look to others.

Living with a touchy Threat system can make you feel on edge, jumpy and exhausted.

It can affect your memory and learning, and make it harder to relax and enjoy yourself, or focus on anything other than your appearance.

 Pause and Think **5 Minutes**

Observe your Threat system

Answer the following questions about your Threat system.

How 'touchy' is your Threat system? What happens in your body when it is set off? What feelings does it bring?	
What situations in the outside world often set off your Threat system?	
Do the Body Bullies show up and trigger your Threat system with unkind words or by calling you names? How do you feel when they appear? How does this affect your actions?	

 Try This **5 Minutes**

Turn down your Threat system

Try to see your Threat system as an over-sensitive alarm rather than something bad. If a smoke alarm is set off by burnt toast, you don't have to throw the alarm in the bin! Instead, you can check if there's a fire, and if not, turn it off and get on with your day.

Use **Notice the NOW** whenever you need to create a pause and turn down the volume of your Threat system.

Notice your Threat system has switched on and how it is affecting your body and mind.	I'm feeling anxious, embarrassed and angry. My heart is thumping, my stomach is churning and my face feels hot. I'm having thoughts about how bad my skin is and how everyone was staring at me in class today.

Observe your body and the world around you. Name two or three things that you can see, hear, feel, taste and smell. Take three slow breaths from deep in your belly, noticing all the sensations.	I can see a green book. I can hear traffic outside the window. I can feel a smooth water bottle in my hands. I can press my feet into the floor and stretch my shoulders. I can smell and taste the cookie I am eating. I feel my belly swelling and cool air in my nose as I breathe.
What's important? What's next? Once your Threat system has started to settle down, it's time to check in with your Guide and make Wise choices without getting pulled into unhelpful Appearance Actions.	I'm going to get back to studying and focus on my work. I will talk to my sister and ask about her day. I'll go for a walk and notice the colours and sounds outdoors.

If anxiety and an over-sensitive threat system are a big issue for you, we talk about this more in our book: *10 Minutes to Beat Anxiety and Panic.*

Holly: My Threat system kicks in whenever I think about the girls from school. Cruel Critic shows up and says I'm a waste of space because I don't look right and I'll never be liked or accepted. I spend so much time trying to perfect my hair and make-up, but the Body Bullies always say that it's just not good enough. It's exhausting!

I tried using Notice the NOW yesterday evening when I was stressed about going to school. It wasn't easy but afterwards, I felt a bit calmer. I managed to pull myself away from the mirror and asked my sister to bounce on the trampoline with me. We lay there and chatted, and it was nice to hang out without thinking about what I looked like.

 **Read This** **10 Minutes**

Drive system

Your Drive system motivates you to get things done. It encourages you to seek out what you need and want, like friendships, food, treats or success in school and sports. Whenever you pass a test, win a competition or achieve a goal, your Drive system kicks in, giving you feelings of pleasure, excitement and satisfaction.

The Drive system helps you focus on important goals and build relationships. When balanced with the other systems, it boosts your confidence and self-belief and leads to success in many areas of life.

However, if things get out of balance, problems can arise. If you use your Drive system too much, you reach 'over-drive' where you are too focused on tough goals without allowing enough time to rest or have fun. You become exhausted, have trouble relaxing and struggle with sleep. This can also happen if you spend too much time on unhelpful Appearance Actions like mirror checking.

On the other side, if you feel low or depressed, you may cut down on meaningful or enjoyable activities. This leads to 'under-drive' where you are not activating your Drive system enough. This makes you tired and demotivated and makes your mood and confidence worse still.

 Pause and Think **10 Minutes**

Balance your Drive system

Answer these questions to help create balance in your Drive system.

When have you used your Drive system? Can you think of a time that you achieved something, even very small? How did it feel to do this?	
Is your Drive system balanced? Do you push yourself too hard to get things done, or are you over-focused on appearance-related activities? Or are you stuck in under-drive where it's hard to get anything done? How does this affect your mood or your sense of achievement?	
Ask your Guide and Wise Mind: Can you try to create more balance in your activities? Keep all your values in mind, such as enjoyment, relaxation or connection.	

Plan a micro-step: Can you plan a small, achievable goal to activate Drive positively? Turn back to Chapter 8 if you need a reminder of how to do this.	

 **Read This**   **5 Minutes**

Be kind to yourself

Having high standards, like 'I like to look my best' and 'It's important to try hard' can give you a sense of accomplishment and boost your self-esteem. However, if these expectations are impossibly high or if you expect everything about your appearance to be perfect, you may be setting yourself up for failure.

Comparing yourself to digitally enhanced images on social media can also be damaging. Living with unfair or unrealistic targets creates pressure, stress and anxiety. Your confidence can plummet, and you may start to believe that you're not capable of looking right or being 'good enough'.

 Pause and Think   **10 Minutes**

Can you treat yourself with more kindness?

Here are some of our tips for ways to treat yourself with more kindness and use your Drive system wisely. How could you use these ideas?

Relax your expectations: Let go of unrealistic demands and aim for 'good enough' rather than perfection. Can you aim for silver or bronze rather than a gold medal? What would this look like for you?	
Do things for fun: Engage in activities because they are interesting or fun, not to try and sculpt your body or because you are striving for achievement or praise. For example, plan to be more active during the week without setting specific goals about distance or speed.	

Choose activities that feel good: This could be dance, sport, yoga or creative hobbies that make you feel good about your body's abilities. It's about the joy and fulfilment they bring, not how you look while doing them.	
Set health-focused goals: Plan to eat balanced meals and exercise regularly to feel better and be healthier rather than focusing on how it will change your appearance.	

Holly: My Drive system has become all about my appearance – I spend so much time and energy trying to look better that I've stopped doing a lot of other things. When I feel down, I go into 'under-drive', shutting myself away in my room and cutting myself off from the world. I'm going to set some micro-goals that have nothing to do with how I look. I used to relax by sketching anime drawings, so I might get my book out and give it a try for a few minutes. I might also message my friend to meet up – she's fun and she never seems to care about how she looks – it would be great to see her!

 **Read This** **10 Minutes**

Calm and Connect system

When your Calm and Connect system is active, you feel relaxed, your heart rate slows and you feel calm, peaceful and safe. It helps you recover from stress, settle strong emotions and quiet the Body Bullies. This system also helps you connect with those who care about you, bringing feelings of affection and soothing difficult emotions. There are many ways to activate this system. It might be the comfort of a friend's hug after a tough day or relaxing in a warm bath with calming music.

When struggling with appearance concerns, your Calm and Connect system often gets under-activated because you are spending so much time using the Threat and

Drive systems to focus on your looks. Without the balance this system provides, you can develop intense feelings of shame and sadness, along with painful and self-critical thoughts brought by the Body Bullies.

It can also be a problem if your Calm and Connect system becomes linked to the Threat system. This can happen if those who are supposed to care for you are also frightening or abusive. Behaviours and emotions usually associated with safety and care can trigger fear instead. An example of this could be if you are experiencing bullying and criticism from people who call themselves your friends.

 **Read This** **10 Minutes**

Meet Cruel Critic

Cruel Critic often shows up when the Calm and Connect system is turned down too low. This Body Bully exaggerates flaws in your appearance and calls you hurtful names. This constant negativity can lead to feelings of sadness, shame and a loss of self-esteem.

 Try This **10 Minutes**

Supercharge your Calm and Connect system

Listening to Cruel Critic can trigger many distressing and painful feelings, including embarrassment, shame, guilt and sadness. However, you can counteract this by plugging in your Calm and Connect system and giving it a 'supercharge' that helps you be kinder and more encouraging to yourself. Here are some ways to do this.

Supercharge your Calm and Connect system	How can you use this? What can you do?
Connect with a supportive tribe: Spend time with those who encourage and support you. Who makes you feel safe and accepted? Who values you for more than just your appearance?	

cont.

Supercharge your Calm and Connect system	How can you use this? What can you do?
Try a calming activity: Spend 5–10 minutes on a relaxing activity such as taking a bath, reading, knitting, doing a jigsaw, yoga, colouring, painting or stroking your pet.	
Go into nature: Take a few minutes to appreciate the outdoors. Look at the sky, a tall tree or a beautiful view. Use your senses to experience the moment – notice what you can see, hear, feel and smell.	
Practise your Open and Observe skills: Being present and mindful strengthens your Calm and Connect system. Take a few slow breaths or practise relaxation techniques. You can turn back to Chapter 7 for more ideas.	

 **Read This** **10 Minutes**

Being a friend to yourself

Activating your Calm and Connect system involves using your Wise Mind and becoming a good friend to yourself. Here's how:

→ **Be friendly and encouraging:** Be kind and understanding to yourself. Accept who you are and set fair, realistic expectations. Remember, you're not supposed to be superhuman or perfect, but just doing your best in a complicated world.

→ **Remember you are not alone:** Many people share similar feelings and concerns. Focus on your strengths, abilities and achievements. You are defined by much more than your appearance.

→ **Observe what's happening inside:** Step back and notice any uncomfortable thoughts and feelings without getting stuck or fixated on them. These are not the only ways to view your appearance! Turn back to Chapter 9 for some ways to do this.

→ **Choose kind actions:** Plan caring micro-actions, like making a relaxing drink or choosing a healthy snack. Don't let these get squeezed out because you are busy, feeling down or are caught up in Appearance Actions.

→ **Stand tall:** Use your body posture to show that you matter. Notice and speak up when situations or people lack respect, equality or care for you and others.

 Pause and Think  **10 Minutes**

Become your own best friend

Look at the table below for some ways that you can switch on your Calm and Connect system and treat yourself with kindness.

Become your own friend	Examples of what to try	Can you use this? What could you do?
Have a friendly and encouraging attitude.	Put a sticky note on your mirror as a reminder to be kind to yourself. Use the same words to talk to yourself as you would to a friend. Send yourself a friendly text message for a boost.	
Remember you are not alone.	Reach out to someone you trust. Try a new hobby or volunteer your time to help others in a positive environment. Find a supportive online group based on your interests, not appearance.	

cont.

Become your own friend	Examples of what to try	Can you use this? What could you do?
Observe what's happening inside.	Take a few slow breaths as you notice and name any difficult thoughts and feelings. Place a hand over your heart or wrap your arms around your shoulders and give yourself a hug with warmth and kindness. Remind yourself: This is a tough moment. I'm on your side. You can get through this.	
Choose kind actions.	Spend a few minutes doing something enjoyable: read, draw, sit in the park, practise yoga, take a bath with scented oil, massage your hands with cream or spend time with loved ones.	
Stand tall.	Stand upright and grounded, like a mountain or a tree. Create a calm space and express your feelings and values calmly. Set boundaries and say 'no' to activities or relationships that make you feel bad about your appearance. Call out discrimination or injustice.	

Holly: I want to be a better friend to myself. I'm always nice to other people, but I never treat myself that way! I've put sticky notes on my mirrors, reminding me not to spend too long staring at my appearance and to be kinder to myself. I'm going to hang out more with people who treat me with respect. I'm thinking about trying a street dance class. Everyone there seems to be more interested in dancing than worrying about their looks, and they wear cool street clothes rather than tight leotards. I'm also going to stand tall, remember what matters to me and put effort back into my studies. I won't let those girls stop me from doing what I care about or getting a job I enjoy in the future.

Summary: treat yourself kindly

➔ Saying negative things about yourself is just as hurtful as saying it to another person.

➔ Three emotion systems affect your body, mind and emotions:

> Threat helps you react to danger with Fight Flight Freeze actions.

> Drive motivates you to achieve goals and get things done.

> Calm and Connect helps you feel peaceful and safe, and recover from stress.

➔ Being a friend to yourself means being encouraging and friendly, setting fair expectations and choosing kind actions that take care of you.

Final thoughts

Make a note of anything you have found helpful, interesting or surprising from this chapter.

....

....

....

....

....

....

What are you going to do now? Can you choose one small action based on what you have discovered?

....

....

....

....

....

....

Chapter 12

HEALTHY LIFE HABITS

Building healthy life habits involves finding daily routines that help you feel confident and comfortable in your own body, without being caught up or fixated by your appearance. This is about finding a balance that works for you. Being physically active is positive and enjoyable, but it's less healthy to push yourself so hard that you become exhausted. Similarly, having a daily skincare routine can keep your complexion glowing and healthy, but spending a vast amount of time or money on cosmetics, and only being satisfied with completely perfect or blemish-free skin, can leave you feeling stressed, frustrated and fearful of not living up to these unrealistic standards. It is also important not to neglect caring for your body altogether.

In this chapter, we will explore how creating a balanced routine with healthy life habits and good self-care can boost your body confidence and wellbeing.

These habits include:

- → healthy eating patterns

- → being physically active

- → getting enough sleep

- → body health and hygiene

- → making healthy choices such as not smoking or vaping, limiting alcohol, avoiding drugs and reducing over-use of technology and social media.

Noah: At first growing taller and broader felt great. I felt strong and did well in sports. I started training every day after college, taking protein shakes and energy drinks to bulk up faster. I loved watching my muscles grow and getting attention at the gym. But then I overdid things. I pushed myself until I was exhausted and in pain, and I started getting injuries from lifting too heavy. I became so focused on my appearance that I stopped enjoying my workouts. It never felt like I was doing enough or that I was big enough. I even started skipping meals and just having protein shakes. My dad kept saying I wasn't getting the right nutrition for my growing body and we argued for the first time ever.

 Pause and Think   10 Minutes

What are your life habits right now?

Unhealthy life habits like poor sleep, lack of exercise or an unhealthy diet, can have a negative effect on your immune system, leave you feeling tired, irritable, fed up and sluggish, and make it harder to do things that are important or enjoyable. They can also affect your body image and confidence.

Take a moment to think about your current life habits. What's helpful or healthy for you? Is there anything that you would like to change or improve?

Life habits or patterns	What are you doing already that's healthy or helpful?	What would you like to change or improve?
Healthy eating: Do you have regular eating patterns and a balance of healthy nutrition that works for your body and lifestyle? Are you able to keep a healthy weight?		
Physical activity: Are you active or do you spend a lot of time sitting or lying? How much exercise do you carry out each week?		

Sleep: Do you have regular sleep habits and usually wake up feeling rested? How easy is it to drop off? Do you stay asleep through the night?		
Health and hygiene: Do you have any health conditions to care for? Do you take medication, use creams or care for your health in other ways? Do you have a personal hygiene routine?		
Other life habits: Do you have any unhealthy habits such as smoking, vaping, drinking too much alcohol or taking drugs? Do you have healthy technology or screen habits?		

 Read This    10 Minutes

Healthy eating habits

Jasmine: When I'm worried about my appearance, I often feel sick or bloated. Sometimes I see my belly sticking out of my jeans like a muffin top, so I've started skipping meals. But then I get super-hungry and end up eating junk food or crisps for a quick fix. They fill me up for a bit but then I just feel cranky and irritable. Lately, I've been tired and breaking out in spots. I think my eating patterns are a big part of this. I know it's important to eat well for my long-term health, but I just want to lose that bulge.

Healthy eating is important for your body and mind. A balanced diet supports growth, helps maintain a healthy weight and provides the energy you need for daily activities. Good nutrition strengthens your bones, muscles, skin, teeth and hair. It also lowers the risk of conditions like heart disease and type 2 diabetes, setting the foundation for lifelong health.

Healthy weight can look different for everyone and it's important not to focus too much on measuring how heavy you are or on your body size – these are not always accurate reflections of your overall health. It's more important to aim for a balanced and healthy diet that includes a variety of foods from different food groups in roughly the right proportions. You don't need to achieve this with every meal, aim for a balance over a day or week. It may help to imagine your plate as a circle divided into sections, each representing a different food group.

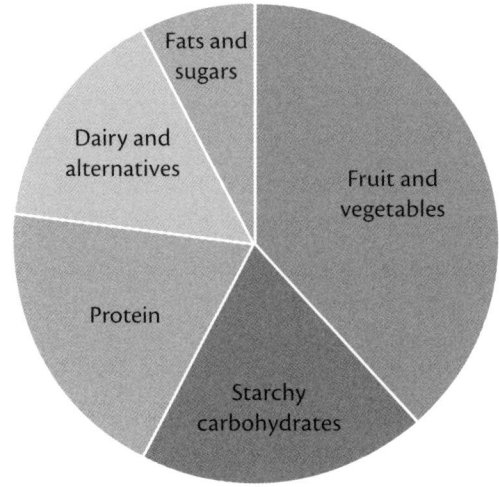

 **Read This** **5 Minutes**

Eating and emotions

When you are feeling anxious or low, you may lose your appetite, stop enjoying food or experience bloating or pain after eating. Some people turn to food as a comfort for emotional distress, often craving sugary or high-fat junk foods. If this becomes a habit, it can affect your overall health. Not eating enough, or avoiding certain types of food, can lead to tiredness, headaches or dizziness, making it harder to stay active and healthy.

On the other hand, food and cooking can be enjoyable and a great way to care for your body. They also help you connect with others, so developing healthy habits can bring many benefits.

 Read This  5 Minutes

Eating disorders

For some people, eating can be a source of great distress and can be linked to a distorted body image or extreme appearance concerns. Recognizing an eating disorder is crucial, as it affects both physical health and emotional wellbeing. Common eating disorders include anorexia nervosa, bulimia nervosa and binge eating. These disorders are not always visible through changes in your weight.

If eating makes you feel anxious, guilty or upset, or you are restricting your food intake or changing your eating patterns because of difficult emotions or concerns about your appearance, it is important to seek help. Effective treatments are available. Talk to your doctor or a trusted adult, and look at the resources section of this book for useful links.

If eating is a topic that you find triggering or distressing, feel free to skip this section and explore other healthy life habits.

 Pause and Think 10 Minutes

Creating healthy eating habits

Look at the following checklist to see our tips for ways to balance your eating habits.

Healthy eating habits	What can you continue doing? What do you need to change?
Food is fuel for body and brain: Eat regular meals to keep your body fuelled with nutrients without peaks and troughs of energy. Don't skip meals, and have healthy snacks if you are using more brain or body power.	
Get involved: Planning and cooking meals can be fun and gives you more control over your food choices. It's a calming activity that allows you to immerse yourself in the smells, tastes and sensations. Why not experiment with a new dish or ingredient?	

cont.

Healthy eating habits	What can you continue doing? What do you need to change?
Include whole grains and fibre, like wholewheat pasta, brown rice and wholemeal bread, and keep the skin on potatoes and root vegetables for energy and gut health.	
Eat a rainbow: Different coloured fruits and vegetables provide essential vitamins and minerals. Aim for at least five portions each day.	
Include protein with each meal: Add fish, meat, poultry, eggs, pulses, seeds or nuts to promote muscle strength.	
Drink water with every meal and throughout the day, which hydrates you and helps balance your appetite and food intake. Avoid sugary soft drinks or fruit juice.	
Limit processed foods: Keep a limit on processed foods high in sugar, fat or salt like fizzy drinks, crisps, cakes and chocolate. Enjoy them occasionally and in small amounts.	

Make mealtimes social: Create a habit of regularly eating with your family. Turn meals into a time to talk as well as to eat. How about banning mobile phones from the dinner table?	
Avoid unnecessary supplements: A balanced diet provides all the nutrients you need. Supplements, protein shakes and energy drinks should only be used if advised by a health professional for specific conditions.	

Jasmine: I started getting more involved with preparing food and began reading labels to see which foods are nutritious. I was shocked at how much sugar is in some breakfast cereals! Cooking with my mum has made it easier to chat with her, and mealtimes have become more of a family event.

I still enjoy treats now and then like chocolate and ice cream, but cutting down on junk food has made me feel better – my stomach is less bloated, and I have more energy.

 **Read This** **10 Minutes**

Physical activity

Physical activity has many health benefits. It strengthens muscles and bones, helps maintain a healthy weight and can reduce the risk of illnesses like heart disease, cancer and diabetes.

Exercise releases 'feel-good' hormones that make you calmer and happier. It boosts energy and reduces stress, irritability and worry. Being active, especially outdoors, can improve your sleep. It is also a social activity and a great way to develop friendships through shared interests.

Exercising your body builds confidence and self-esteem, and can strengthen your concentration, memory and thinking skills. You can use short bursts of activity to break up long periods of studying or sitting.

 Pause and Think   10 Minutes

How do you feel about physical activity?

Appearance concerns can affect the type or amount of activity you choose, or trigger thoughts or emotions that make it harder to be active. Answer the questions below about your attitude to physical activity.

Do appearance concerns affect how much physical activity or exercise you do, or influence the type of activity that you choose?	
Do the Body Bullies stop you from being active or do they push you to do too much exercise? What would happen if you followed their negative advice about activity?	
What skills can you use from other GROWTH chapters to start making physical activity part of your routine?	

 Pause and Think   10 Minutes

Different types of physical activity

Different people prefer different types of physical activity. It's important to look for things that you enjoy, as well as find ways to bring more physical movement into your daily routine and reduce how long you spend staying still.

Types of physical activity	Does this interest you?	What could be the next step? How can you bring this into your life?
Walking, hiking or increasing your step count/speed		
Martial arts, trampolining or gymnastics		
Cycling, jogging or athletics		
Dance, yoga or Pilates		
Skateboarding, ice skating or rollerblading		
Strength training, going to the gym or circuit training		
Swimming or water sports		
Ball sports such as football, tennis or basketball		
Outdoor activities such as climbing, horse riding, paddle boarding or sailing		
Physical work such as gardening or working outside		
What other types of activity can you include?		

Pause and Think    **10 Minutes**

Physical activity for body confidence

Making regular physical activity one of your healthy life habits is an important way to improve your body image, build your health and fitness, and befriend your body. Here are some ways you can do this.

Physical activity habits	How could you use this? What will you do?
Create a routine: Make physical activity a regular part of your life. Can you combine it with something you already do, like walking to school or work, or heading to a sports club on your way home?	
Start slowly: Set small, realistic goals to build up your activity. Even standing more rather than sitting is a start! What might be a micro-step to get you moving? A 10-minute walk can build up to a jog, as you gradually increase the speed and distance. Avoid over-ambitious targets that put you off starting.	
Make it fun: How can you make getting active more enjoyable? Plan a fun day out with friends, walk your dog, learn a new dance routine or try geocaching. Can you listen to music or a podcast while moving? Experiment with new activities to build your skills and confidence.	
Make it social: Exercising with friends boosts motivation and enjoyment. Who can you invite for a walk, join at the gym or take to a dance class? Can you join an outdoor activity group like Scouts or Guides? Do you like team sports?	

Boost your mood: Physical activity helps with stress and energizes you, especially when done outdoors. Find out what works best for you – whether it's a peaceful solo swim or a jog, or walking and talking with a close friend.	
Expect setbacks: Don't let these throw you permanently off track. If you're busy, tired or injured, reduce your activity but try not to stop completely. Gradually build up again when you are ready.	

 Try This **5 Minutes**

Next steps for physical activity habits

What are your next steps to create healthy activity habits?

....

....

 **Read This** **10 Minutes**

Healthy sleep habits

Noah: I was drinking energy drinks loaded with caffeine and sugar to try to boost my performance at the gym, but they just made me feel jittery and wired. I was also working out late at night, which made it hard to wind down. Before bed, I'd spend ages on social media, scrolling through photos and videos of bodybuilders or influencers with huge muscles. That made me feel stressed and insecure and made it hard for me to relax or fall asleep. I started feeling tired at college, and I missed a few deadlines. Once I even dozed off during a class! I had dark circles under my eyes and even my friends noticed I wasn't my usual happy self. I realized things had spiralled out of control and it was time to make a change.

We all need good sleep. It's essential for rest, growth and overall wellbeing. Most young people aged 11–24 need around 8–10 hours of sleep per night. Lack of sleep or poor-quality sleep can negatively affect your mood, stress levels, performance, concentration, creativity, weight and immunity.

Worries about your appearance or problems in life like exams, homework, friends or work can make it hard to sleep. You might find it tough to fall asleep or wake up early thinking about these issues, leaving you tired in the morning. Worrying about not sleeping enough can also make you anxious and keep you awake at night.

What affects sleep?

Your body clock: Your sleep is regulated by your body's internal clock or circadian rhythm, which is influenced by light, temperature, activity and eating patterns. Bright light keeps you alert, while darkness triggers the release of hormones like melatonin, which makes you feel sleepy.

During the teenage years, your body clock shifts, causing you to stay up and wake up later. Try to keep consistent activity and sleep patterns throughout the week, and don't try to catch up on missed sleep at weekends. Getting outside in daylight hours helps keep a good rhythm.

Stimulants: Caffeine, nicotine, alcohol and drugs can interfere with sleep. These stimulants are often found in energy drinks and supplements. While alcohol and certain drugs might initially make you sleepy, they can cause early waking and poor-quality sleep.

Technology and social media: Late-night use of social media, messaging or gaming can make you agitated and wakeful. Screens emit blue light, which can trick your body into thinking it's daytime, making it harder to fall asleep.

How is your sleep?
An occasional poor night's sleep is normal. But, if you've been struggling with sleep for a few weeks or more, it's time to identify the causes and make changes. Start by tracking your sleep amount and quality over one or two weeks.

Day/Date						
What time did you go to sleep?						
What time did you wake up?						
Rate the quality of your sleep from 1 to 10. How rested or energetic did you feel afterwards?						
Notes: What things might have affected your sleep (helpful or unhelpful)? Was there any change to your routine?						

 **Read This**  **10 Minutes**

Top tips for improving sleep

There are many things you can do to improve your sleep. Look at the list below to see whether these tips might help. Can you choose two or three things to try?

I have trouble getting to sleep.	**Set a regular sleep routine:** Balance your body clock by sticking to consistent bed and wake-up times. Avoid sleeping in, even after a bad night or at weekends.
	Create a wind-down routine: Engage in relaxing activities like reading, listening to music, taking a bath or yoga. Avoid social media or gaming at least an hour before bed.
	Make a 'sleep haven': Ensure your bedroom is dark, quiet, uncluttered, comfortable and at a good temperature for sleeping.
	Cut out daytime naps: Occasional short naps are OK, but avoid making this a habit. If you must nap, keep it under 15 minutes and before 3 pm.
	Reduce stimulants: Avoid caffeine, nicotine, alcohol and energy drinks, especially within six hours of bedtime. Avoid eating heavy meals late at night.
	Cover the clock: Set the alarm and don't keep checking the time, which can cause anxiety and worry.
I have trouble staying asleep and wake in the night.	**Sleep when tired:** Only go to bed when you feel sleepy to avoid lying awake frustrated.
	Get up and try again later: If you are still awake after 20 minutes, get up and do something calming until you feel sleepy again. Repeat if necessary.
	Use your bed for sleep: Have a separate desk or work area and switch off phones and computers or keep them out of the bedroom.
I have trouble waking up, or I wake up exhausted.	**Get daylight exposure:** Try to spend at least 30 minutes outside in daylight, especially in the morning.
	Stick to your routine: Get up at your usual time, even if tired. A refreshing shower or a gentle stretch may help.
	Regular physical activity: Exercise helps you feel tired naturally and improves sleep quality.
I'm kept awake by negative thoughts or worries.	**Journal your thoughts:** Writing down thoughts, dreams or worries in a journal or notebook can clear your mind and help you see things differently.
	Use problem-solving: If something is troubling you, write it down and try to think of solutions or make a to-do list well before bedtime.
	Avoid sleep battles: Stressing about sleep keeps you awake. Try to accept a bad night and focus on self-care the next day.

Technology or social media affects my sleep.	**Limit late-night electronics:** Avoid screens and activities that make you alert or stressed like social media or watching the news.
	Charge your phone elsewhere: To stop messages and notifications interrupting sleep, charge your phone in another room.
	Dim the screen: Use night mode with warmer tones in the evening.
	Relax with audio: Listen to audiobooks or music instead of watching screens before bed.

 Try This **10 Minutes**

Next steps for better sleep

What are your next steps to create healthy sleep habits?	
What small changes might help improve your sleep routine? Could you increase daytime physical activity, or plan a calming bedtime routine where you relax in a warm bath each evening?	

Noah: Using the sleep diary helped me to notice some of my unhealthy habits! I started charging my phone in the hall at night, so I was less tempted to check it and start scrolling. I also cut back on late-night gym sessions. Now I work out straight after college and focus on enjoying myself and staying healthy rather than pushing myself to exhaustion. I've cut back on energy drinks, especially in the afternoon and evening, which has helped my sleep. I'm eating more meals with my dad and having regular food has given me more energy. I'm definitely feeling better!

 **Read This** **10 Minutes**

Other health and hygiene habits

During puberty and the teen years, your body changes in many ways. You might experience a growth spurt, with changes in height, weight and body hair. Increased oil production can make your skin greasy and prone to spots or acne. You may sweat more and develop body odour. Girls will start menstruating and need to adopt new menstrual hygiene habits. Dental hygiene is also crucial, especially if you wear braces.

If you have a long-term condition like diabetes, asthma or epilepsy, you may need to follow specific health advice. This might include taking medication, using inhalers, monitoring your blood or applying creams. Mental health issues like anxiety, depression or eating disorders can also affect your body image, as can neurodivergence such as autism, ADHD or dyslexia. These can make you feel different or make you struggle with social acceptance.

It's essential to take care of your body well without going to extremes. Avoid using harsh chemicals, washing too frequently or having an overly complicated skincare routine, as these can harm your skin and increase anxiety about your appearance.

Whatever your health issues, adjust your habits to suit your unique needs. Follow medical advice and find health and hygiene habits that bring feelings of pride, confidence and acceptance of your body.

 Pause and Think **10 Minutes**

Next steps for health and hygiene

What are your next steps to create healthy healthcare and hygiene habits?	
Have you been neglecting your health and hygiene habits? Or have your habits become extreme and take up too much time and attention?	
What small changes could improve these habits?	
How could you remind yourself? Can you create a routine or set a reminder? Can you 'habit stack' and link the change to something you already do, such as cleaning your teeth?	

 **Read This** **2 Minutes**

Healthy technology habits

Living in a digital age brings many benefits, but it can also be challenging to manage screen time. Overuse of technology can harm your productivity, memory, creative thinking and sleep.

Technology becomes a problem when it distracts you from important tasks or conversations. Excessive screen time reduces physical activity, and comparing yourself to others on social media can cause anxiety and affect mood and body confidence.

The goal is to balance technology use with other aspects of life, following your Guide and making wise choices about how you spend your time.

 Pause and Think **10 Minutes**

What are your technology habits?

How much time each day or week do you spend using technology or online? It may help to use a screen time tracker to record this.

Complete the table below.

Technology habits	How many hours each day or week?
Working or studying online	
Using social media	
Playing computer games	
Sending messages or pictures to others	
FaceTime or video calls	
Other types of technology	

Now ask yourself:

What do you notice in your technology habits? How is technology contributing positively to your mood or self-esteem?	

Do your technology habits take up a lot of time or distract you from other important parts of life?	
Do you use technology to avoid difficult feelings?	
Do you need to make any changes in your technology habits? What might be the first step?	

Drugs and alcohol

Drug and alcohol problems can cause physical and emotional damage. If you are affected, it's important to recognize the problem and seek help. Talk to a trusted adult or your doctor if these have become an issue for you.

Summary: healthy life habits

→ You can improve your mood and body confidence by creating healthy life habits that include eating habits, sleep, physical activity and health and hygiene.

→ Cut back on unhealthy choices like smoking, excessive alcohol, drug use and overuse of digital screens.

→ Prioritize and repeat healthy actions until they become routine.

Final thoughts

Make a note of anything you have found helpful, interesting or surprising from this chapter.

....

....

....

....

....

....

What are you going to do now? Can you choose one small action based on what you have discovered?

....

....

....

....

....

....

Part 3

BOOSTING YOUR BODY CONFIDENCE

Chapter 13

MAKING FRIENDS WITH YOUR BODY

Logan: My classmates say I look odd and make weird comments. I know I think and act differently from them. My brain just works differently. It hurts when I get teased or bullied about my looks. I often feel lonely and isolated and that I don't fit in. I don't want to shut myself away from the world. I want to be able to brush off negative comments, stand up for myself and be confident in my body. I want to accept myself and enjoy doing the things I love.

In this final section, we'll explore ways to boost your confidence and self-belief. Think back to why you picked up this book. What challenges are you facing, and what do you want to change? How can you use GROWTH skills to handle difficult thoughts and feelings and improve your body confidence?

We've looked at factors affecting body image and discovered what can get in the way of being who you want to be and doing the things you want to do. We've learned skills to face difficulties, accept your appearance and appreciate your body's capabilities. Now it's time to put it all into action.

In the final chapters, we'll cover:

➜ coping with strong or distressing emotions and thoughts of self-harm, related to body image

➜ boosting confidence by applying GROWTH skills to boost body-confident actions

➜ expressing your thoughts and opinions through body-confident communication.

 **Read This** 🕐 **10 Minutes**

What do we mean by body confidence?

Confidence includes body confidence and body acceptance. It means believing in yourself and your abilities, knowing that you can achieve what matters to you. Self-esteem is also important, which involves feeling good about yourself and believing you're worthwhile. Body confidence includes celebrating your unique body, appreciating your strengths and understanding that your worth is not defined by your appearance.

Confidence doesn't mean you're perfect or can't make mistakes. It comes from being kind and accepting who you are, especially when life is tough, things don't go to plan, or your appearance isn't exactly as you'd like. It also means cutting down on how often you compare yourself to others and becoming comfortable with your body.

Confidence helps you to face whatever life throws at you, encouraging you to seize new opportunities rather than shy away. This increases your chances of reaching your full potential and succeeding. The good news is that many GROWTH skills can boost your body confidence. If you've been practising the skills and tips in this book, you might already feel more confident. Now it's about putting these skills into action.

Body confidence and strong emotions

Struggling with self-esteem, confidence or self-worth, can lead to powerful and distressing emotions like shame, sadness, fear or self-disgust. These thoughts or emotions may feel overwhelming and lead to thoughts of self-harm. If this happens, seek support and keep yourself safe. We'll discuss strong emotions and self-harm in Chapter 14, and there are links provided to seek support at the end of the book.

Body confidence in challenging situations

No one feels confident all the time. Some situations might make you feel less confident, especially in social settings or when the focus of attention is on you. Building confidence involves facing challenging situations rather than avoiding them. This involves stepping outside your comfort zone and choosing body-confident actions. Can you start to become more willing to 'give things a go' without being too hard on yourself if you don't succeed right away? You can use your GROWTH skills to cope with any uncomfortable thoughts and feelings that pop up when your confidence is low. We'll cover this in Chapter 15.

Body-confident communication

Improving your communication skills is an important way to boost confidence. Communication includes your words, body language, posture and tone of voice. Confident communication can improve your relationships and confidence in social situations, showing that you respect yourself and others. This helps you stand up for your rights and assert yourself when needed.

How you talk to yourself also matters. Use Wise Mind as a supportive and encouraging coach rather than listening to negative messages from Body Bullies like Cruel Critic. This helps you face challenging situations with greater confidence, believing in your own worth.

We will look at body-confident communication in Chapter 15.

 Pause and Think  **10 Minutes**

How body confident are you?

First, let's check in to see what your body confidence looks like. Read the following checklist and rate each item from 1 to 5 (where 1 = not at all and 5 = strongly agree).

Confidence and self-acceptance	How much do you agree with this? (1 = not at all, 5 = strongly agree)
On the whole, I am satisfied with myself.	
I feel that I'm equal to others.	
I think my appearance is OK.	
I feel OK when attention is on me.	
I can do things as well as most other people.	
I feel that I have many good qualities.	
I acknowledge things I do well.	
I have respect for myself as a unique individual.	
I accept myself and my flaws.	
I appreciate my body and can focus on the positive aspects of my appearance.	
I never deliberately put myself down.	
I have a positive attitude towards myself.	
I feel comfortable in my body and posture.	
I accept it when I make mistakes and believe I can learn from them.	
I talk to myself in a positive, encouraging way.	
Total score (out of 75)	**/75**

Now answer these questions.

What was your score? The higher the score, the more self-confident you are likely to feel. Does this match how you feel inside?	
Which situations help you feel more confident, believe in your abilities and accept your body and appearance?	
Which situations or people make you feel less confident?	
How confident are you in talking to others or standing up for yourself?	
What do you need to work on to improve your body confidence?	

Summary: making friends with your body

In this chapter, we explored some ways to make friends with your body so you can build body confidence.

➜ Body confidence involves accepting and celebrating your unique body.

➜ You can learn to appreciate your body whilst also understanding that your worth is not defined by your appearance.

➜ You can become kinder to yourself and cut down negative comparisons with others.

In the next few chapters, we will explore ways to boost your body confidence, even when coping with strong emotions, and learn some skills in body confident communication.

Final thoughts

Make a note of anything you have found helpful, interesting or surprising from this chapter.

....

....

....

....

....

....

What are you going to do now? Can you choose one small action based on what you have discovered?

....

....

....

....

....

....

Chapter 14

COPING WITH STRONG EMOTIONS

Harper: There were times when I felt really bad about myself. After looking at pictures on social media, I would stare at myself in the mirror and feel disgusted with my appearance. It got so bad that I started feeling the urge to harm myself. Cutting myself became a way to cope with the overwhelming emotions and numb the pain. Every day became a battle, trying to hide it from my parents and pretending everything was fine. Seeing the scars just made me feel even worse and more ashamed. I didn't know where to turn.

Living with body image and appearance concerns can trigger intense emotions and lower your self-esteem. You might even have thoughts about harming yourself. For some, self-harm becomes a way to cope with distressing thoughts and feelings.

At times, it may feel hard to keep going, and you may even think about ending your life. These thoughts can happen to anyone and don't mean you will act on them. They will often pass as your mood improves again.

If you are experiencing thoughts or urges to harm yourself or end your life, it's a sign you need support and care. Talk to someone you trust, like a parent or teacher, or a health professional such as your doctor or school nurse. You could also contact support lines like Childline or the Samaritans. Links to these are provided at the end of the book.

Remember, talking about suicidal thoughts or self-harm won't make you more likely to act on them. Sharing how you feel might help you find better ways to cope with difficult emotions.

In this chapter, we will:

➜ learn to recognize when strong feelings are starting to appear

→ discover ways to cope with powerful emotions without resorting to harmful patterns of behaviour

→ learn how to make your situation safer by creating a safety plan.

 Pause and Think **5 Minutes**

Spot the warning signs

Thoughts about self-harm or suicide usually show up when there are strong emotions, so it's helpful to recognize how this feels. This way, you can notice when you are starting to feel upset and take action before you feel overwhelmed.

Here are some examples of thoughts, feelings, body sensations and urges you might have when you're really distressed. Mark any that you've noticed in yourself, and add anything else that's important.

Feelings	Hurt, guilt, sadness, shame, despair Frustration, anger, rage, hatred Panic, anxiety, fear, dread Any other feelings:
Thoughts	This is unbearable. I can't deal with this. I'll never look as good as others. Nothing will get any better. I can't stand feeling this way. Nothing will help. I must stop feeling this way. Any other thoughts:
In your body	Tired, heavy, crying, thumping heart, tight chest, restless, fidgety, burning or pain. Any other body sensations:

 Pause and Think **10 Minutes**

Notice your Emotion Traps

How do you react to strong or difficult feelings? It's common to fall into 'Emotion Traps'. These are actions that may seem helpful at first but will often make you feel worse over time. Check out these examples – do any seem familiar?

Emotion Traps	Do you recognize this? Yes/No	Does this action help you in any way? How?	Does it cause problems or make things worse for you? How?
Appearance Actions, such as checking in the mirror, trying to hide how you look or avoiding others			
Injuring yourself or causing yourself pain, such as by cutting or scratching your body			
Shouting, yelling or arguing with friends or family			
Silently accepting abuse, harsh criticism or body shaming from others			
Sleeping or spending a long time in bed to avoid feeling bad or facing the world			
Avoiding important activities because they make you distressed, tired or anxious about your appearance			
Binge eating, eating unhealthy food or not taking care of yourself			

 Read This  10 Minutes

Self-harm

Self-harm is when you deliberately damage or injure your body. This can include cutting, scratching, burning, punching, pulling out hair or taking an overdose. It can also include risky behaviours, such as provoking fights or unsafe sex. Self-harm can affect anyone, regardless of age, social status, gender identity, sexuality, race or culture. There are many reasons why people self-harm, but for many, it's a way of attempting to control or get relief from strong or overwhelming negative emotions.

Negative body image can be an important trigger for self-harm. Dissatisfaction with your appearance can cause feelings of contempt or shame that create an urge to harm yourself. Other stresses can also contribute, such as relationship issues, bullying, money worries, exam pressure or coming to terms with your sexuality or gender. Self-harm may also be a way to cope with trauma, such as abuse or the death of someone close. Feelings of low self-worth might make you feel powerless, making it hard to speak up in protest or express your feelings.

Usually, self-harm is not an attempt to end your life, but it does increase the long-term risk of suicide, especially if it continues. Self-harm is an expression of distress and should be taken seriously. People who self-harm require support, compassion and care for any injuries. If you are experiencing distress, it is important to tell someone and to seek help. There are some resources and organizations at the back of this book that may help.

 **Read This**  **10 Minutes**

Thoughts of suicide

Strong emotions, such as feeling ashamed, disgusted or depressed about your body or appearance can trigger extreme negative thoughts. You might feel hopeless, thinking that you'll never fit in and that no one cares. These thoughts can seem very convincing but are not accurate or realistic ways to look at yourself or your future. They are simply a sign of deep distress.

Thoughts about suicide should always be taken seriously. Seek help and support to cope with these feelings or any problems in your life.

 **Pause and Think**  **5 Minutes**

What's true for you?

Do you ever experience thoughts of self-harm or ending your life?	

Which feelings are most likely to trigger these thoughts?	
Do you ever act on these thoughts by harming yourself in any way?	
What circumstances are most likely to lead to you thinking and feeling this way?	

 **Read This** **5 Minutes**

Finding your way through

If you're feeling overwhelmed or having thoughts of self-harm or suicide, remember there are ways to cope with your problems and any painful thoughts and feelings. You don't have to feel stuck or alone. Talking to someone you trust can help until the difficult feelings pass.

In an emergency, call 999 for an ambulance or go to Accident and Emergency. If you overdose on tablets, it is important to be seen quickly in the hospital, as this can be very dangerous. For non-life-threatening situations, contact your doctor or phone 111 for urgent advice.

There are many helplines, text and online chat services available for emotional support. Check the support section at the back of this book for more information.

 **Read This** **10 Minutes**

Make space for difficult feelings

When you are hit by strong emotions like fear, anger or shame, it can be hard to think clearly, and you may react in ways that make things worse. Remember, these feelings are temporary and will pass if you give them space and time. It's like finding a tree to shelter under during a heavy rainstorm. You might still get a little wet and cold, but the tree offers protection and a chance to catch your breath before moving on.

You don't have to change or get rid of difficult feelings right away. Use Open and Observe skills to pause and keep yourself safe while waiting for the emotional storm to pass. Notice and name what's happening inside you. This can help you step back and feel less overwhelmed so you don't fall into the usual Emotion Traps.

Name a difficult feeling

Next time you have a strong or distressing feeling, try just naming it in a friendly and caring way.

Name the feeling.	I'm feeling angry, sad, scared and ashamed.
Observe the feeling: how does it affect your body and mind?	There is tightness in my chest and burning in my stomach. I want to clench my fists, shout or throw something!
Be a friend to yourself: use your Calm and Connect system.	This is a tough moment. It feels really bad right now, but it won't last forever. It's like a storm cloud – and it will pass by soon! I can get through this – I believe in myself!

You could also try using the Notice the NOW exercise from Chapter 2.

Improve the moment

When you're feeling distressed or overwhelmed by strong emotions, finding small ways to improve the moment can help. This means stepping out of the uncomfortable feeling and shifting your attention to a different activity. Even micro-steps may make it a little easier to cope. Improving the moment isn't about ignoring negative thoughts or feelings but means creating space and time to find better ways to react. You can return to the problem later when you feel a little better.

Look at the list of activities below that might help improve the moment when you notice strong emotions. Underline anything you'd like to try and add other activities in the space provided. Think about what might help in different situations. Then choose two or three examples to experiment with and see what happens.

How to improve the moment	Examples	Could you try this? What will you do?
Exercise and activity	Go for a walk, jog or bike ride, walk quickly up the stairs, stretch or do yoga, jump up and down, rip some paper or stretch your body.	
Be creative	Draw, paint or sculpt, dance, write in your diary, sing, play a musical instrument, knit or sew.	
Connect and communicate with others	Phone or message a friend, sit with a family member, go to a public place, have a hug, talk to someone you trust or call a helpline.	
Relax or find a little calm	Take a bath or shower, stroke a pet, have a warm drink, give yourself a hand massage, listen to music or a podcast, do slow breathing, smell your favourite perfume and imagine a safe place.	
Be constructive	Build or make something, spend 5 minutes organizing your room, mow the lawn, wash the dishes, make someone a present, write a 'to-do' list or volunteer your time.	
Focus on something else	Watch a TV programme, do some homework, play a computer game, do a puzzle, watch a funny video, do something that makes you smile or laugh.	
Look after yourself	Paint your nails, apply body lotion, put on a nice outfit and have a healthy meal.	

cont.

How to improve the moment	Examples	Could you try this? What will you do?
Release tension	Clench an ice-cube, sprint for 30 seconds on the spot, draw lines on your skin with a red pen, snap a band on your wrist, punch a pillow and listen to loud music.	
What else can you try?	What other examples can you think of?	

 Try This **10 Minutes**

Make a CRISIS safety plan

It's very helpful to make a safety plan for ways to stay safe when you are experiencing distressing or risky thoughts or urges. Remember that you are doing this because you want to take care of yourself and because you are worth the effort. The safety plan steps can be summarized by the word CRISIS:

→ **C**alm strong feelings

→ **R**easons for living

→ **I**deas for getting through tough times

→ **S**afer Space

→ **I**nterrupt or distract yourself from difficult thoughts, feelings or urges

→ **S**eek help and **S**upport.

Steps of a CRISIS safety plan	Ideas and questions to think about	How could you use this? What could you try?
Calm strong feelings	What might help you feel less distressed and lift your mood? Consider calming activities like Notice the NOW, taking a shower, going for a walk or writing in a journal.	

Reasons for living	Who or what do you appreciate or care about? Think of people or animals that you want to live for. Include names and photos to remind yourself during difficult times.	
Ideas for getting through tough times	What might make it easier to cope with strong emotions? Make a list of what's helped and keep it handy, like on your phone. Cut down on alcohol or drugs, which can make it harder to resist thoughts of self-harm or suicide.	
Safer **S**pace	How can you make your surroundings safer? Remove items you might use to harm yourself, like blades or excess medication. What people or places make you feel safer? Try creating a safe space at home, where you never self-harm and go there if you are feeling overwhelmed.	
Interrupt or distract yourself from difficult thoughts, feelings or urges	How can you distract yourself from negative thoughts or urges to self-harm? Create a pause or delay by keeping yourself busy, doing physical activity or being around others.	

cont.

Steps of a CRISIS safety plan	Ideas and questions to think about	How could you use this? What could you try?
Seek help and **S**upport	Who can you reach out to if you are distressed or thinking about self-harm? Write down the names and phone numbers of: → friends and family for support → local and national helplines (online, phone or text) → health professionals like your doctor, mental health team or A&E.	

Harper: At first, I didn't know what to do or who to turn to, but I decided to tell my form tutor about my self-harm and worries about my appearance. I felt embarrassed and awkward, but she was really kind and understanding. It was a big relief to share how I was feeling and to know that someone wanted to help. She convinced me to talk to my parents and it does feel better now there are no secrets at home. They were upset at first but have been supportive and encouraged me to see a counsellor. My mum helped me create a CRISIS safety plan, and if I start feeling overwhelmed or upset, I look at it to remind me what to do. I threw away all the things I was using to scratch my skin so I'm less tempted when I'm upset. We made a safe space in the living room with cushions where I can go if I'm feeling stressed, and I find it helps to listen to loud music that drowns out negative thoughts.

 Read This    5 Minutes

Speaking out about body shaming

Being bullied, criticized or body-shamed can trigger strong emotions and distress. You may feel that you have little control over the situation and resort to self-destructive actions, such as passively accepting abuse or self-harm.

While you can't always stop others from criticizing you, you can control how you respond. Speaking out about how you feel and communicating your thoughts and feelings directly and honestly can help you cope with body shaming.

Not all feedback is meant to be unkind. Sometimes negative thoughts brought by the Body Bullies may influence how you interpret neutral or even positive comments, so you see them as harsh or critical. If this sounds like you, revisit Chapter 11 to learn how to treat yourself with more kindness.

For practical tips to handle harsh feedback, criticism or body-shaming remarks, see Chapter 16.

Summary: coping with strong emotions

→ Strong emotions are only temporary and will pass if you give them space and time.

→ Seek help if you have thoughts or urges to harm yourself or end your life.

→ Talking about these feelings won't make you more likely to act on them and can be the first step to feeling supported and safer.

→ Use a CRISIS safety plan to help you stay safe during times of intense or negative emotions.

→ Speaking out and dealing with criticism, body shaming and bullying can help you feel more in control of your emotions and reactions.

Final thoughts
Make a note of anything you have found helpful, interesting or surprising from this chapter.

....

....

....

....

....

What are you going to do now? Can you choose one small action based on what you have discovered?

....

....

....

....

....

Chapter 15

BOOSTING BODY CONFIDENCE

Suri: I just want to be able to do the things I enjoy and get on with my life. I'm fed up with always being worried about how I look or what others think about me. I want to be more confident and stop beating myself up about my appearance. I'd love to be able to believe in myself and my abilities.

When you lack body confidence, you might retreat to places where you feel safe, avoiding challenges and missing out on activities that bring purpose and achievement. The Body Bullies often act like party spoilers, telling you, 'This is too scary!' or 'You look ridiculous!' If you let these negative thoughts control your choices, life becomes restricted and dull. It's like getting stuck on a narrow path surrounded by thorns, focusing only on avoiding scratches rather than cutting through the undergrowth and clearing the path.

You don't have to believe the Body Bullies! The best way to boost your confidence is to step outside your comfort zone and face challenges using your GROWTH skills. This helps you cut through the bushes that are keeping you stuck on that narrow path and will open up many new views and opportunities.

Building confidence also helps you stay on track rather than giving up when things get tough. By tackling challenges, you start to feel stronger and more capable. Successfully dealing with one problem makes the next one easier to face as you tell yourself, 'I did it before – I can do it again!' This creates more opportunities for enjoyment and growth.

In this chapter, we will:

→ explore the confidence zones and discover ways to move from the Comfort Zone into the Stretch and Growth Zones

→ use your GROWTH skills to take confidence-boosting actions that give you a sense of achievement and satisfaction.

 Read This ⏰ **10 Minutes**

Explore the confidence zones

Building confidence involves stepping just outside your comfort zone. Let's look at the different confidence zones:

Comfort Zone: This is where you feel safe and secure, facing few challenges. It's great for resting and relaxing but spending too long here means missing out on opportunities. You might avoid challenges and stick to activities that you can do easily, which can become boring and make you fearful of change. Constantly avoiding what you fear can shrink your confidence and self-belief.

Stretch Zone: Taking small steps outside the Comfort Zone moves you into the Stretch Zone. Here, you are taking small risks and trying new things. You experiment with life, test out what happens when you make changes and learn from your experiences. As you move into the Stretch Zone, new possibilities open up and your confidence grows. You start saying, 'Yes I can try this!'

Growth Zone: In the Growth Zone, you fully commit to learning new skills and developing your abilities. You take bigger steps away from the Comfort Zone towards important goals. Your confidence in learning and adapting to challenges increases. You also become skilled at bouncing back from setbacks, finding solutions and creating new pathways to success.

Overload Zone: In the Overload Zone, you have taken on a challenge that feels a little too overwhelming and difficult. Your confidence may dip, causing stress and anxiety, and your performance might suffer. It's wise to avoid reaching this zone when setting goals to maximize your chances of success and keep your confidence high. However, if you do reach this point, it's not a disaster. Recognize what has happened and drop to the Growth or Stretch Zone. Try to avoid retreating to your Comfort Zone as this can hinder progress towards your goals.

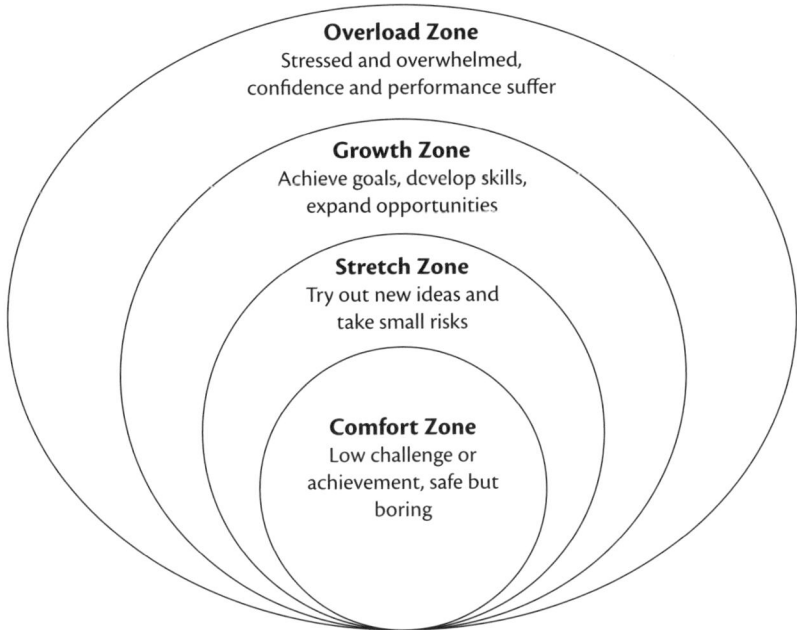

 Pause and Think   **10 Minutes**

Look at the description of the confidence zones and then answer these questions.

What are you currently doing that's within your Comfort Zone?	
Is there anything you want to do but don't feel confident enough to try? What is it?	
What situations/people or places do you avoid because of your lack of body confidence?	
What opportunities to expand your skills and what goals are you missing out on by avoiding situations/people and places?	

Here's what Suri said:

What are you currently doing that's within your Comfort Zone?	I feel comfortable at home with my family. They dress casually and care more about working hard and achieving than about looks.
Is there anything you want to do but don't feel confident enough to try? What is it?	My college friends often go out at weekends, but I worry that I wouldn't fit in or look as good as them.
What situations/people or places do you avoid because of your lack of body confidence?	When they invite me, I make excuses not to go out at weekends. I'll just feel underdressed and awkward.
What opportunities to expand your skills and what goals are you missing out on by avoiding situations/people and places?	I would like to spend more time with my friends, and maybe even find a boyfriend. I wouldn't neglect my coursework, I just want to have a bit more fun in my free time.

 **Read This**    **10 Minutes**

Confidence-boosting and confidence-draining activities

Building body confidence is about taking action to step outside your comfort zone. You don't have to wait until you feel more confident to do this! You can take small risks and behave 'as if' you feel just a little more confident.

Confidence-boosting activities are small actions that move you into the Stretch Zone and then towards the Growth Zone. Make sure these are micro-steps, so they do not push you too far or too fast, and avoid reaching the Overload Zone. In contrast, confidence-draining actions are those that keep you stuck or make you feel less confident about your abilities.

Here are some examples.

Confidence-boosting actions:

➜ small actions that give a sense of achievement or satisfaction

➜ actions that are important or meaningful to you

➜ not being over-focused on your appearance or how you look

➜ involve a wide range of your skills and abilities.

Confidence-draining actions:

➜ avoid trying things due to fear of 'failure' or 'not looking right'

- → reduce your opportunities and keep you stuck or trapped

- → push yourself too far too fast

- → over-value the importance of your body or appearance.

 Pause and Think **10 Minutes**

What actions are **confidence boosters** that move you into the Stretch Zone and the Growth Zones?	
Which actions are **confidence drainers**, zapping your confidence, making it all about appearance and moving you back towards the Comfort Zone?	
What people, places or activities help to boost your body confidence?	
What would you do differently if you felt more confident? Can you do some of these things anyway? Behaving 'as if' you feel more confident can help to build your confidence over time.	

 **Read This** **3 Minutes**

Using GROWTH skills to boost your body confidence

Change is not easy, especially when the Body Bullies are telling you how scary it would be to leave the Comfort Zone or that you're not good enough to do it. Building confidence will help you embrace new and exciting opportunities and reach your full potential. Let's explore how you can use the GROWTH skills you learned in Part 2 to boost your confidence in many different situations.

Pause and Think **10 Minutes**

Guide yourself towards confident choices

Confidence comes from knowing who you are and who you want to be. Build your confidence by making choices that follow your Guide and reflect the 'real' you. Let others see you for who you really are – including any mistakes, insecurities and imperfections – rather than trying to hide these or acting in a way that's not true to you.

Turn back to Chapter 7 and remind yourself about your Guide. Make a note of three or four important values here.	
Are your values balanced and are you focusing on what really matters? Are you neglecting or ignoring any important values?	
How can you choose wise actions that build your confidence and bring these values to life by planning small steps into the Stretch Zone?	

 Try This **10 Minutes**

Get ready to take confident actions

It's usually easier to try to *act* with confidence, rather than to *feel* confident. It doesn't matter if you sometimes feel anxious or have inner doubts. Try not to compare yourself harshly to others. You can never judge how confident another person feels just by looking at them. Many people seem confident on the outside but doubt themselves inwardly or may worry about their appearance without showing it.

You can choose confident actions, even if you feel anxious or uncertain. By behaving 'as if' you feel more confident, you may start to feel more confident too. Even if your feelings don't change, acting confidently will help you achieve what matters to you.

Taking confident actions involves:

→ **developing skills and knowledge:** invest time and effort to achieve goals or take part in activities that you care about or want to improve in

→ **trying new experiences:** experiment with new ways of doing things to move into the Stretch Zone

→ **taking part in challenges:** participate in tests, performances, expeditions and competitions to move into the Growth Zone

→ **problem-solving:** use inner strengths to handle obstacles, preventing you from falling back into the Comfort Zone.

How to stretch your confidence	Examples of confidence stretching in action	What might you try?
Stretch or improve an existing skill or learn something new.	*I like tennis and I'd like to try playing with someone new. I could join an acting group or a debating club.*	I will…
Try new hobbies and interests.	*I've always wanted to learn about coding … photography … car engines … singing … I'm going to join an online course or a local group.*	I will…
Take part in challenges such as tests, performances, competitions or expeditions.	*I'm going to challenge myself to audition for a part in a drama performance. I'm going to push myself to pass the next level in my ice-skating class. I'm going to sign up for an exciting expedition that takes me abroad.*	I will…
Take the lead by organizing or running things.	*I'm going to stand for class representative or to be on the school council. I will volunteer to fundraise for a school project.*	I will…
What else can you think of?		I will…

 **Read This** 🕐 **3 Minutes**

What gets in the way of taking confident actions?

Planning confident actions and taking small risks can trigger difficult feelings like fear, anxiety or doubt. You might also experience body sensations, such as butterflies in your stomach, tension or a pounding heart. These can be uncomfortable and may tempt you to retreat to the Comfort Zone.

Think about a situation where you lack confidence. Imagine yourself in this situation, about to take a risk or try something new. Ask yourself 'What uncomfortable thoughts, beliefs, feelings, sensations or urges make it harder to step outside my Comfort Zone?'

This is where you have a *choice* – stay stuck in the Comfort Zone to avoid these feelings, or experience a little discomfort and follow your Guide into the Stretch Zone. Use Open and Observe skills to cope with any uncomfortable feelings. Remember, these will usually fade as your confidence grows.

Now visualize yourself using Open and Observe skills to make room for difficult feelings and successfully cope with this difficult situation. See yourself staying strong and coping well. Congratulate yourself for your strength and ability to handle difficulties.

 **Read This** 🕐 **10 Minutes**

Listen to your Wise Mind

Confidence can also stem from your inner conversations and the stories you tell yourself. Doubts, negative thoughts and fears can all become major obstacles to success. Body Bullies like Gloomy Gaze or Cruel Critic can undermine your confidence by blaming you for problems or calling you names. Fears about failure, mistakes or rejection may all stop you from choosing actions that help you grow. However, avoiding difficult situations only reinforces these unhelpful beliefs and knocks your confidence even further.

On the other hand, listening to your Wise Mind helps you solve problems, overcome obstacles and build confidence. Can you let your inner coach guide and support you as you make wise choices that help you achieve important goals, even when life seems uncertain, or your confidence wavers?

 **Try This** 5 Minutes

Tune in to Wise Mind

Imagine the voices of the Body Bullies and Wise Mind are coming out of different earphones.

In the left earphone, you can hear the harsh voices of the Body Bullies. Cruel Critic is making spiteful comments about your appearance, and they are all telling you to stay in the Comfort Zone and avoid doing things you care about.

From the right earphone, you can hear the voice of Wise Mind and your inner coach. Wise Mind is giving you encouragement and support, being positive, boosting your confidence and bringing you courage.

Can you turn down the volume of the left earphone and tune into Wise Mind on the right? What might Wise Mind be saying? What wise actions can you take if you take out the left earphone altogether and follow your Guide?

 **Read This** 5 Minutes

Treat yourself kindly

To improve and learn, it's important to be able to seek constructive and supportive feedback from others. This can help to move you from the Comfort Zone into the Stretch or Growth Zones. When doing this, remember to treat yourself kindly and use your Calm and Connect system to motivate and encourage growth. If you constantly listen to a harsh inner critic, rather than an encouraging inner coach, you may react defensively to feedback, making it harder to learn. It's also crucial to be kind to yourself when you are experiencing repeated criticism or bullying, or if you are struggling with self-acceptance.

 **Pause and Think** 10 Minutes

Think about a situation where you would like to stretch yourself to move out of your Comfort Zone into the Stretch or Growth Zones.

How could you use kindness to create resilience and motivate yourself to overcome obstacles and make these changes?	
What attitudes or phrases could you use?	
What kind of actions might encourage you to be brave, embrace change and grow your confidence?	
If you make a mistake, what supportive words can you use to learn from it and try something different?	
How does it feel to motivate yourself with kindness rather than criticism or blame?	

 **Read This**  **10 Minutes**

Healthy life habits

Sticking to healthy routines can create stability and boost your confidence. Life often involves setbacks – maybe you develop a new spot right before an important presentation, have a sleepless night before an exam or feel anxious and sweaty as you prepare to go to a party. Nevertheless, building resilience means getting up again after you fall, being flexible and trying different approaches when things go wrong. Healthy habits can help you bounce back and maintain your wellbeing. When life is uncertain, rely on these routines to stabilize and care for yourself.

Pause and Think  **5 Minutes**

Which healthy life habits are most helpful when you are facing problems or uncertainty? This might be a habit of physical activity, healthy nutrition or trying to limit unhealthy choices that bring down your mood and knock your confidence further.

Summary: building body confidence

In this chapter we have learned:

→ Getting stuck in the Comfort Zone feels safe but can make life boring and limit opportunities.

→ You can plan and carry out confidence-boosting actions even if you feel a little anxious or unsure.

→ Moving into the Stretch and Growth Zones will build your confidence as you try new things and learn from experience.

→ Motivate yourself with kindness and avoid pushing yourself too far or too fast to stay out of the Overload Zone.

Final thoughts
Make a note of anything you have found helpful, interesting or surprising from this chapter.

....

....

....

....

....

....

What are you going to do now? Can you choose one small action based on what you have discovered?

....

....

....

....

....

....

Chapter 16

BODY-CONFIDENT COMMUNICATION

Avery: My friends are important to me, and I want to fit in and have fun. That includes my style of clothes. My parents never approve of what I'm wearing, and they always make negative comments about my fashion choices, hair colour and make-up. We often have arguments before I go out, which leaves us all feeling upset and frustrated. I don't want to keep having rows or disrespect my parents, but I also want to feel like an individual and have some choice about what I wear and how I look. I want to feel body confident and to have my own style!

Improving your communication skills is crucial for building confidence. This involves not just your words but also your posture, tone of voice and overall appearance. Being body confident means expressing yourself through confident actions and body language. This helps you handle tough situations, negative comments and external pressures by what you say, how you act and how you present yourself.

Body-confident communication includes recognizing your strengths, treating yourself kindly, overcoming negative self-talk and standing up to negative inner voices like the Body Bullies. The GROWTH skills from Part 2 will help with this.

In this chapter, we'll learn to:

➜ develop a confident posture and body language

➜ use confident communication skills that help you to talk to yourself and others with understanding and respect

➜ respond effectively to criticism or body shaming and learn to say 'no'.

 **Pause and Think**  **10 Minutes**

How confident is your communication?

Let's check in to see how confident you feel in your communication skills. Look at the following checklist and rate each item from 1 to 5 (where 1 = not at all and 5 = strongly agree).

I can say 'no' if I don't want to do something.	
I can pay attention and focus on listening when I am talking to someone.	
I am comfortable looking at someone when they are talking to me.	
I can tell my friends how I feel.	
I can accept helpful feedback from others.	
I can stand up for myself if other people say things that are unfair or unkind.	
I can ask for help if something is difficult or upsetting me.	
I can give and accept compliments.	
I can tell others if I disagree with them.	
I can speak confidently without mumbling or stumbling over my words.	
Total score (out of 50)	**/50**

Now answer these questions.

What was your score? The higher the score, the more confident your communication is likely to be. Does this match how you feel inside?	
Which situations help you communicate more confidently?	
Which situations or people make this more difficult?	
What do you need to work on to improve your body-confident communication?	

 Read This  10 Minutes

Confidence and rights

To build confidence and self-belief, it's crucial to understand your rights. We all have legal rights that protect us from discrimination and harassment. Nevertheless, sometimes you may feel that your rights are being restricted or ignored. You may have faced inequality or unfairness from your family, peers or society, perhaps around important issues like gender, race, class or disability.

Beyond legal enforcement, embracing your rights involves believing in and accepting yourself. This ties in with body confidence, which we explored in Chapter 15. Remember, everyone is equal and entitled to their rights. This mindset can boost your confidence and self-belief.

 Pause and Think  10 Minutes

Consider your rights!

Look at this list of rights and then answer the questions below:

→ I have the right to express my feelings, opinions and beliefs.

→ I have the right to be treated with respect and fairness.

→ I have the right to set boundaries and say no.

→ I have the right to follow my interests and passions.

→ I have the right to make mistakes and learn from them without being judged.

→ I have the right to ask for help and support when I need it.

→ I have the right to stand up against discrimination and unfair treatment.

→ I have the right to feel safe in my environment.

→ I have the right to take time for myself and look after my own needs and wellbeing.

→ I have the right to be proud of who I am, regardless of what others think.

Now answer these questions:

Which of these rights do you agree with? Can you think of any times that you have acted on or lived by these?	
Have you ever felt that any of your rights were not respected? How did that make you feel?	
Are there any rights that you find hard to assert? What gets in the way?	
What small actions could you take to help protect or act upon one or more important rights?	

 **Read This**  **5 Minutes**

Confident body language

You can tell a lot about how someone feels from their posture and actions. This includes many of the unhelpful Appearance Actions we read about in Chapter 4. Do you try to hide parts of your body with your hands or clothing because you lack body confidence?

Communication isn't just verbal. Your eyes, facial expression, voice, posture and clothes all send signals, which can make you seem confident and strong, or passive and unsure. Neglecting self-care and appearance can suggest unhappiness or a lack of self-respect.

Behaving 'as if' you feel good about your body can enhance your self-belief. Adopting a confident posture can create a positive feedback loop in your brain, making you feel more confident. Even holding a 'Superhero Pose' for a few minutes daily can help build this habit.

 **Try This**  **2 Minutes**

Check in with your body language.

How are you sitting right now? Notice your posture and how you are holding your body. Are there any body sensations such as tightness or discomfort? What are you wearing? How does this fit with where you are and what you are doing at this moment?

How confident and comfortable in your body do you feel right now, from 1–10 (1 = not confident and 10 = complete confidence)?

If the number is lower than 7, is there anything you could change to make yourself feel more confident?

 **Pause and Think** **10 Minutes**

Body language

There are many ways that you can express confidence through your body language. Not everyone is the same, so it is important to find your own comfortable body language. Look at the following table to see if there is anything you recognize or would like to try.

	Body-confident body language	**Passive, aggressive or indirect body language (try to avoid this!)**
Posture and movement	Stand upright with open chest and shoulders. Lean in slightly when listening. Stay close but don't crowd the person you are speaking to. Use open, relaxed hand movements and gestures.	Covering your mouth, hunching shoulders, crossing arms, pointing fingers or clenching fists. Standing too close or above someone. Not paying attention, sighing or looking bored.
Eye contact	Keep a steady eye contact and occasionally look away.	Staring aggressively, looking downwards or completely avoiding eye contact.
Facial expression	Match your expression to your emotions (smiling when pleased, frowning when concerned). Keep your jaw relaxed.	Sarcastic laughter, smirking, exaggerated expressions or fixed false smiles.
Speech pattern and voice	Speak at a steady pace, with a clear, warm tone and varied pitch.	Shouting, talking loudly, speaking very softly or using a monotonous tone.

cont.

	Body-confident body language	Passive, aggressive or indirect body language (try to avoid this!)
Self-care and clothing	Wear clothes that demonstrate confidence and suit the situation, reflecting your values and personality.	Neglecting hygiene, hiding body parts with dark or baggy clothes, wearing outfits that are inappropriate for the situation, or overly sexualized.

These are not fixed rules and it's important to adapt your body language to suit your personal needs and preferences rather than just trying to fit in with what society may expect. This is especially true for neurodivergent individuals. An autistic person may find it stressful or distressing to make eye contact with others, and someone with sensory difficulties may feel more at ease and comfortable wearing loose or baggy clothes. Focus on what is right for you. The aim is to find your own unique body language that helps you feel stronger and more confident in social situations.

 Pause and Think **10 Minutes**

Now answer these questions.

Can you recognize any unhelpful patterns of body language in yourself?	
What small changes could you make that might build your confidence and help you express yourself more clearly?	

 **Read This** **10 Minutes**

Communicate with confidence!

Humans developed verbal communication to build friendships, connect with others and form social groups, which are essential for survival. However, communication can sometimes lead to conflicts and misunderstandings, causing frustration and isolation.

How you dress and present yourself is a form of self-expression, which can sometimes cause disagreements with parents, teachers or cultural leaders who may have different views. You may also need to match your appearance to specific situations, like wearing a school uniform. It's important to respect others' opinions, rules and customs while staying true to yourself and your values. This can be difficult and may lead to conflicts.

Confident communication involves talking to yourself and others with understanding and respect. It can improve relationships, resolve conflicts and boost your confidence. It allows you to stand up for yourself while respecting others. It's not about overpowering others or winning arguments through aggression or force. Instead, it's about expressing your views calmly and negotiating outcomes that respect everyone's viewpoint.

Confident communication is based on three principles:

1. **Equality and respect.** Everyone deserves to be respected, heard and understood and to hold their own opinions and views (including about appearance and clothing!).

2. **Common humanity.** Focus on what you have in common with others rather than your differences to foster understanding and reduce conflict.

3. **Empathy and compassion.** Understand your own and other people's feelings and concerns. Show kindness and understanding to build connections and relationships.

 **Read This** **10 Minutes**

Four steps to confident communication

The four steps of confident communication can be summarized as **NEAR**. To communicate and build confidence, you need to get closer to others with fairness, kindness and connection, rather than avoid others or distance yourself from people, groups or situations. The four steps are:

1. **N**otice what is happening in the situation and describe it without judgement.

2. **E**motions: recognize how you are feeling and express yourself to others (if you wish).

3. **A**sk yourself what matters to you and the other person.

4. **R**easonable request – what can you ask for that might help meet your needs?

You can use these steps to help you listen and respond to others, as well as in how you talk to yourself and deal with the Body Bullies or your negative thoughts.

Step 1: Notice and describe what is happening without judgement

Everyday communication often involves sharing your views and opinions about a situation, which may involve analysing, judging or criticizing others. This can cause disagreements and create distance between people.

A better approach is to describe the situation factually and without judgement. Check with the other person if your impression is correct and try to understand their point of view. This reduces the emotional 'sting' from communication. Here are some tips:

→ Describe what happened in simple sentences.

→ Say what you saw or heard.

→ Express yourself clearly and honestly.

→ Avoid judgements, interpretations, blame or instant demands.

 **Pause and Think**   **10 Minutes**

Look at these examples of different ways to communicate.

Judging, blaming or criticizing	Describing the situation
It was a disgusting morning, and my day was ruined because my hair got wet and I looked like a drowned rat!	There was a lot of rain this morning and my hair got wet.
You are so rude. It's impossible to talk to you about anything!	You spoke in sharp sentences and your tone seemed angry when I said your jacket looked nice.
You're a liar and an awful friend. You never make any effort to include me.	I noticed you posted on social media from the party, although I thought you had said you didn't want to go.
I'm so useless in class, I never speak up for myself.	I didn't say anything when the teacher asked what topic we wanted to study next.
You obviously don't care about what's happened.	Your expression suggests to me that this doesn't bother you … is that right?

 **Try This**  **10 Minutes**

Now practise coming up with phrases that describe what you see or hear, show understanding and respect someone else's view, or state a preference. You can use these for self-talk or when talking to others.

Pitfalls to avoid	What not to say	What could you say instead?
Judgements, criticisms, insults	You are so irritating when you keep interrupting me.	I notice you are speaking at the same time as me, which makes it hard for me to finish what I'm saying.
	You are such a poser in photos!	
	He is always so lazy.	
	She looks stupid.	
	You are an embarrassment.	
Blaming others or yourself	I'm such a loser, no wonder nobody wants to hang out with me.	
	I always mess things up, I shouldn't have even tried.	
	It's your fault I missed the deadline for my homework because you kept distracting me.	
Undermining someone's opinion or trying to outdo them.	Oh please, anyone could do that...	
	Your idea is stupid. Mine is way better.	
	You think that's bad? I've been through much worse...	
	Whatever, you don't know what you are talking about...	

211

Read This   **10 Minutes**

Step 2: Emotions: recognize and express how you are feeling

The next step in learning confident communication is to recognize and express your feelings. This is not always easy. When emotions are strong or arise quickly you can be caught up in them before you realize what's happened. Spotting your feelings involves asking yourself questions such as:

➜ How do I feel about this?

➜ What's driving my reaction?

➜ What's the worst part for me?

Knowing how you feel can help you to understand what's important and find ways to improve difficult situations. When talking about this to others, use 'I' statements to own your feelings. If expressing your emotions makes you uncomfortable, you can leave out the word 'feel'. Try saying: 'I'm a bit fed up with this situation...' or 'I'm tired and frustrated...'

Your Open and Observe skills can help you to cope with any strong or uncomfortable emotions. You can then use Wise Mind to spot any Body Bullies that have shown up, ask your inner coach to help you find a more balanced and helpful point of view, and find the confidence to express yourself clearly and fairly.

Read This   **10 Minutes**

Step 3: Ask yourself what matters (to you and the other person)

Next, consider what matters most to you and the other person. This involves thinking about your values and needs, like feeling respected or having freedom. You don't need to convince the other person to agree with you right away! The aim is to make sure you hear and understand everyone's perspective. Try asking yourself:

➜ Why is this important to you? Where is your Guide pointing? What values and needs are involved?

→ What might be important to the other person? How would you feel in their position? Is there common ground?

→ What would you like to happen?

During the conversation, tell the other person what matters to you. You can also say things that show you have heard what they have said and that you understand their point of view.

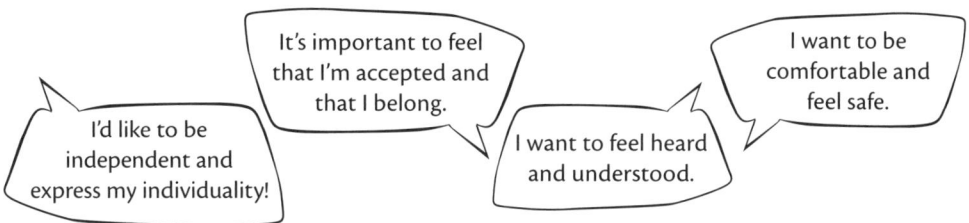

Explore these issues *before* asking for what you want to happen next. This helps you build positive relationships, work together and reduce conflict, making it easier to find creative ways to move forwards, without being stuck on just one solution.

You can turn back to Chapter 7 for more on finding your values and following your Guide.

Read This   **10 Minutes**

Step 4: Reasonable request

The final step is to agree on what to do next, by making a reasonable request. This might involve asking yourself or the other person to do something. A reasonable request only asks for something that the other person can realistically do and respects both your needs and theirs.

A reasonable request is not a demand and doesn't involve control or force. It gives the other person the option to say 'no' without any threat of punishment if they don't agree. Avoid using words like 'should', 'must' or 'ought' as these can lead to conflict or imply that one person is 'right', and the other is 'wrong'.

Here are some examples of demands, preferences and requests.

Demands	Preferences and requests
You ought to…	It would be better if…
You must…	It would be helpful to…
If you don't, the consequence will be…	You could try…
I should always…	I would prefer it if…

To make a reasonable request ask yourself:

➜ How can both your needs and the other person's needs be met? Be creative and think of several possible solutions. Stay flexible until you reach a fair solution.

➜ How can you ask for what you want in a respectful or friendly way that's likely to be received well?

Here are some examples of reasonable requests, take a look and think about how you could use these:

➜ Would you be able to talk more quietly/somewhere more private?

➜ Could you help me understand things better?

➜ Can we agree to have different views?

➜ Can you tell me how you feel about what happened and what you would like me to do differently next time?

➜ Could you give me time to think about what you are asking me to do?

 Read This   5 Minutes

Plan and prepare

Finally, take some time to plan and prepare for a challenging conversation. Think in advance what you want from the conversation and what you plan to say. While you can't control how the other person will respond, it helps to be clear in your mind about the message you would like to convey.

What would be the best time and place to have the conversation? Avoid surprising the person – give them a heads up that you want to discuss something important. Then, 'set the scene' by staying calm and composed. Consider your body language, including your posture, tone and volume of voice, eye contact and even clothing. This preparation can make the conversation go more smoothly.

 Read This   10 Minutes

Here is Avery's example of confident communication in action.

Plan and prepare: Think about the time, place, what you want to say and your body language.	Usually, we end up having a huge argument right before I'm due to go out! Instead, I decided to talk to my parents as soon as I get home from school. I'll still be wearing my school uniform so there's less chance of a fight straight away. I'll start by sharing some good news about my test results. I might even message my mum on the way home to let her know I want to talk about something important.
Notice and describe: Use simple sentences to say what you saw or heard. Avoid judgements, blame or demands.	I've noticed we often argue about the clothes I'm planning to wear when I go out for the evening, and it usually ends up with us shouting and getting upset.
Emotions: Express how you feel using 'I' statements.	I feel hurt and embarrassed when you say I look like a disgrace and tell me to change my clothes or try to stop me from going out. After we argue, I feel guilty and upset at first, but later, it only makes me more determined to do what I want.
Ask yourself what matters: Think about your needs and values and those of the other person. Express both clearly. Ask the person to confirm that you get their point of view.	I know you care about me and worry about my safety and what others think about how I dress. I appreciate everything you do for me, and I love and respect you as my parents. I want us to have a good relationship. Is that true for you too? Staying safe is important to me as well. I always come home at the agreed time, and make sure I'm with a trusted friend when I'm out. I also want to express my individuality through my clothes and to have fun with my friends.
Reasonable request: Express your preference or make a request. Try to find a compromise and avoid making demands.	Can we talk about finding a balance that lets me dress in a way that feels true to me but keeps you from worrying too much? I'd like to discuss this without you saying how bad I look because that hurts my feelings. Maybe we can agree on some rules that we are both comfortable with. I'd really like to feel that you can begin to understand me and how I see the world differently from you.

 **Try This**  **10 Minutes**

Confident communication in action

Choose a situation where you have a slightly difficult message to communicate. Don't pick a huge or complicated problem, start with something that's just a small issue. Use the table to plan how you could approach this using confident communication.

Plan and prepare: Think about the time, place, what you want to say and your body language.	
Notice and describe: Use simple sentences to say what you saw or heard. Avoid judgements, blame or demands.	
Emotions: Express how you feel using 'I' statements.	
Ask yourself what matters: Think about your needs and values and those of the other person. Express both clearly. Ask the person to confirm that you get their point of view.	
Reasonable request: Express your preference or make a request. Try to find a compromise and avoid making demands.	

 Read This 10 Minutes

Coping with criticism

Dealing with criticism or body shaming can be challenging, but knowing how to respond can help maintain your confidence and self-esteem. Criticism about your appearance, or anything else, can be hurtful and may trigger your Threat system, leading to these urges:

→ Fight: You may want to shout or yell, but this may not be helpful or align with who you wish to be.

→ Flight: You might feel like running away, but this prevents you from standing up for yourself and addressing the issue.

→ Freeze: You might become speechless and overwhelmed, leaving you feeling powerless and frustrated.

If your Threat system is triggered or you are experiencing strong emotions, pause and settle these feelings before responding. Take a breath and give yourself a moment to process what was said. This helps you stay calm and think clearly. Turn back to Chapter 14 for ways to soothe strong emotions.

Next, you can turn to Wise Mind to help you respond effectively. Here are some tips.

Pause and ask your Wise Mind	Examples and useful phrases
Is this unkind or unfair? Think about who has spoken – is it a friend, teacher or someone you don't know? Is the comment meant to help or is it just hurtful? Do you want to pay attention to it? If not, disagree firmly.	I don't agree… I don't think that's the case… I think differently… I hear you, but I see it another way… I have a different opinion…
Is it best ignored? Sometimes, the best response is no response. Walk away if the comment is not worth your energy.	I've nothing to say to that… I'm walking away…
Should you stand your ground? If so, politely but firmly let the person know their comment is not OK. Use 'I' statements to let the person know how the comment has affected you.	I don't appreciate comments about my clothes. It's not okay to talk about my body like that. I feel hurt when you comment on my appearance.
Is it partly true? If the comment has some truth, acknowledge it. This shows you are open to feedback, which can strengthen your relationship and enable you to grow.	Thank you for your feedback, I will think about what you have said… I do take a long time in the shower, but I'm not doing it to annoy you or because I'm vain…
Is it constructive? If so, try to accept it and use it as an opportunity to learn and develop. Agree without being dismissive or defensive. Decide if there is something you want to do differently.	You're right, I think that style and colour does suit me better… Yes, I do look fitter since I've been going to the gym regularly…
Would humour help? This can build connection, defuse tension and reduce your own stress.	I'll add that to the list of things I'm not going to do! Do you charge for this advice or is it free?!

 Read This    10 Minutes

How to say 'no'

Learning to say 'no' is important for setting boundaries, managing your time and staying true to your values. It's about respecting yourself and your limits. Saying 'no' is not rude or selfish; it's a way to take care of yourself. True friends and understanding people will respect your decision.

You can use body language to reinforce your body confidence when saying 'no'. Maintain eye contact and speak in a steady, calm voice without shouting. You can shake your head to reinforce your words. Here are some more tips for saying no confidently.

Be direct and clear: You don't need to provide lengthy explanations or excuses. Avoid phrases like 'I'm not sure' or 'I'll think about it', which could be misinterpreted as a 'maybe'.	No, thank you. I can't, sorry. Not this time. No, I'm not interested in doing that.
Take ownership: Use 'I' statements to make it clear that it's your decision. You don't have to defend your choice, but it may help to express your feelings. If you feel the need to explain, keep it short.	I have other plans. I'm too busy today so I won't be able to help. I'm too tired to go out tonight. I can't take on any more right now.
Offer alternatives: If you wish to soften the refusal, you could suggest a different time or another way to help.	I can't do the project today, but I could do it on Saturday. I won't have time to mow the lawn, but I could do the washing up before I leave for school.
Stay polite but firm. If someone is persistent, calmly repeat your 'no'. Stand by your decision without feeling pressured to change your mind.	I understand you really want me to go but I don't have time. Thanks for thinking of me, but I can't help. I appreciate the invite, but I have other plans.

Summary: body confident communication

→ Confident body language includes your posture, eye contact, facial expression, tone of voice and choice of clothing.

→ Confident communication skills help you talk to yourself and others with understanding and respect.

→ The four steps of confident communication involve:

> **N**otice what is happening in the situation and describe it without judgement.

> **E**motions: recognize how you are feeling and express it to others (if you wish).

> **A**sk yourself what matters to you and the other person.

> **R**easonable request – what can you ask for that might help meet your needs?

Final thoughts

Make a note of anything you have found helpful, interesting or surprising from this chapter.

....

....

....

....

....

....

What are you going to do now? Can you choose one small action based on what you have discovered?

....

....

....

....

....

....

Getting Support

Here are some useful organizations you can turn to for support.

UK support

Alumina: Free online 7-week course for young people aged 10–17 struggling with self-harm: www.selfharm.co.uk

Be Body Positive: Support for young people and carers to build positive body image and improve relationships with food: https://bebodypositive.org.uk

Beat Eating Disorders: UK-based eating disorder charity providing information and support: www.beateatingdisorders.org.uk

Child Exploitation and Online Protection: Website run by the National Crime Agency to enable young people to report sexual and other forms of online abuse: www.ceop.police.uk/Safety-Centre

Childline: If you are under 19 you can confidentially call, chat online or email about any problem, big or small: www.childline.org.uk

Cruse: Offering support, advice and information to children, young people and adults when someone dies: www.cruse.org.uk

Harmless: Provides support, information, training and consultancy to people who self-harm, their friends and families and professionals: https://harmless.org.uk

NHS Better Health – every mind matters: Advice and information about mental wellbeing and self-care: www.nhs.uk/every-mind-matters/mental-wellbeing-tips/youth-mental-health

Papyrus: Confidential advice and support for young people struggling with suicidal thoughts or anyone concerned that a young person could be thinking of suicide: www.papyrus-uk.org

Samaritans: Whatever you're going through, at any age, you can contact the Samaritans for support and help in a crisis: www.samaritans.org

Shout: If you are a young person struggling to cope, text YM to 85258 for free, 24/7 support: https://giveusashout.org

The Mix: Online information and a helpline for under-25s offering support for anything troubling you: www.themix.org.uk

Young Minds: UK charity fighting for children and young people's mental health: www.youngminds.org.uk

US and international websites

988 Suicide and Crisis Lifeline: Free and confidential support for people in distress or crisis via text, phone or online chat: https://988lifeline.org

Active Minds: Nonprofit organization supporting mental health awareness and education for young adults: www.activeminds.org

Crisis Text Line: A free 24/7 texting service for young people and adults that can connect you with a trained crisis counsellor: www.crisistextline.org

Mental Health America: Nonprofit organization dedicated to promoting mental health, wellbeing and preventing illness: https://mhanational.org/childrens-mental-health

My Life is Worth Living: Animated online stories focusing on teen characters overcoming emotional challenges such as depression, cyberbullying and fear of disappointing others: https://mylifeisworthliving.org

National Alliance on Mental Illness (NAMI): Resources, information and support for teenagers and young adults dealing with mental health issues: www.nami.org/Your-Journey/Kids-Teens-and-Young-Adults

Recovery Warriors: Support to break free from food and body struggles: https://recoverywarriors.com/

The Trevor Project: Provides crisis support for LGBTQ+ young people by phone and text, as well as information and an international community: www.thetrevorproject.org

Bibliography

Griffiths, C., Williamson, H., Zucchelli, F., Paraskeva, N. and Moss, T. (2018) 'A systematic review of the effectiveness of acceptance and commitment therapy (ACT) for body image dissatisfaction and weight self-stigma in adults.' *Journal of Contemporary Psychotherapy: On the Cutting Edge of Modern Developments in Psychotherapy* 48, 4, 189–204. https://doi.org/10.1007/s10879-018-9384-0.

House of Commons Health and Social Care Committee (2023) *The Impact of Body Image on Mental and Physical Health – Second Report of Session 2022–23*. London: House of Commons. https://committees.parliament.uk/publications/23284/documents/170077/default.

Mental Health Foundation (2019) *Body Image Report –Executive Summary*. London: Mental Health Foundation. www.mentalhealth.org.uk/explore-mental-health/articles/body-image-report-executive-summary.

NHS Digital (2021) *Mental Health of Children and Young People in England 2021 – Wave 2 Follow-Up to the 2017 Survey*. Leeds: NHS Digital. https://digital.nhs.uk/data-and-information/publications/statistical/mental-health-of-children-and-young-people-in-england/2021-follow-up-to-the-2017-survey.

Prazeres A.M., Nascimento A.L. and Fontenelle L.F. (2013) 'Cognitive-behavioral therapy for body dysmorphic disorder: a review of its efficacy.' *Neuropsychiatric Disease and Treatment 2013*, 9, 307–316. www.ncbi.nlm.nih.gov/pmc/articles/PMC3589080/.